CAMBRIDGE LIBRARY COLLECTION

Books of enduring scholarly value

Printing and Publishing History

The interface between authors and their readers is a fascinating subject in its own right, revealing a great deal about social attitudes, technological progress, aesthetic values, fashionable interests, political positions, economic constraints, and individual personalities. This part of the Cambridge Library Collection reissues classic studies in the area of printing and publishing history that shed light on developments in typography and book design, printing and binding, the rise and fall of publishing houses and periodicals, and the roles of authors and illustrators. It documents the ebb and flow of the book trade supplying a wide range of customers with products from almanacs to novels, bibles to erotica, and poetry to statistics.

A Century of Bibles

William John Loftie (1839–1911) wrote prolifically on topics related to travel, art, architecture, and history. In this 1872 work, his stated desire was to investigate those editions of the Authorized Version published in the century following the initial 1611 text. Noting that other historians had 'stopped short' when reaching that acknowledged culmination of English biblical scholarship, he went further, claiming it was 'no exaggeration to assert that our modern Bible is altered throughout from its original, for the better in some places, for the worse in some.' His catalogue and discussion of the various texts involved included those from the British and Bodleian Libraries together with additional lists from scholars Lea Wilson and Francis Fry. Surveying English editions of the Bible published during a sometimes contentious century, Loftie's work reveals how printing and editing practices did, over time, affect even the seemingly static Authorized Version of the Bible.

T0371422

Cambridge University Press has long been a pioneer in the reissuing of out-of-print titles from its own backlist, producing digital reprints of books that are still sought after by scholars and students but could not be reprinted economically using traditional technology. The Cambridge Library Collection extends this activity to a wider range of books which are still of importance to researchers and professionals, either for the source material they contain, or as landmarks in the history of their academic discipline.

Drawing from the world-renowned collections in the Cambridge University Library, and guided by the advice of experts in each subject area, Cambridge University Press is using state-of-the-art scanning machines in its own Printing House to capture the content of each book selected for inclusion. The files are processed to give a consistently clear, crisp image, and the books finished to the high quality standard for which the Press is recognised around the world. The latest print-on-demand technology ensures that the books will remain available indefinitely, and that orders for single or multiple copies can quickly be supplied.

The Cambridge Library Collection will bring back to life books of enduring scholarly value (including out-of-copyright works originally issued by other publishers) across a wide range of disciplines in the humanities and social sciences and in science and technology.

A Century of Bibles

The Authorised Version from 1611 to 1711

W. J. LOFTIE

CAMBRIDGE UNIVERSITY PRESS

Cambridge, New York, Melbourne, Madrid, Cape Town, Singapore,
São Paolo, Delhi, Dubai, Tokyo

Published in the United States of America by Cambridge University Press, New York

www.cambridge.org
Information on this title: www.cambridge.org/9781108010948

© in this compilation Cambridge University Press 2010

This edition first published 1872
This digitally printed version 2010

ISBN 978-1-108-01094-8 Paperback

A Century of Bibles.

A Century of Bibles

or the Authorised Version from 1611 to 1711 to which is added William Kilburne's Tract on Dangerous Errors in the late printed Bibles 1659 with Lists of Bibles in the British Museum Bodleian Stuttgart and other libraries compiled by the reverend W. J. Loftie B. A. F. S. A.

PREND · MOY · TEL · QVE · IE · SVIS

London Basil Montagu Pickering 196 Piccadilly 1872.

PREFACE.

HE many deficiencies of the following list, especially in the Scottish editions and the New Testaments, will be in part supplied by the enumeration in the Appendix of examples in several collections, public and private. The compiler has endeavoured to see every book named in his work: but this was often impossible; and in such cases references are given to the authorities on which they are inserted.

Four sizes have been fixed upon as generally applicable: folio, quarto, octavo, and duodecimo. Quarto and octavo bibles count usually in four signatures and four blanks; in some catalogues, that of the British Museum, for example, the two sizes are often confounded. Some duodecimos, again, count in five signatures and seven blanks, other in six and six; and there is no standard by which to distinguish 12mo. 16mo. 24mo. and 32mo. In the following list, therefore, a rough division is made into "12mo." and "12mo. small," and *this, it is hoped, may ſuffice for the identification of any example.*

The compiler is glad to have this opportunity of thanking Mr. Francis Fry for the kindneſs to which any meaſure of completeneſs attained by the preſent work muſt be attributed. Mr. Fry at one time contemplated forming a catalogue of his own collection, and moſt obligingly gave up the materials he had gathered.

Sir William Cope's loan of his liſt of the Stuttgart collection muſt alſo be warmly acknowledged. It will be found to contain ſome bibles not eaſily identified with any in the preſent work; but the compiler did not obtain it until the greater part of his book was printed.

The books moſt often referred to are, " Cotton's Liſt," 8vo., Oxford, 1852, Second Edition; " Lea Wilſon's Catalogue," 4to., London, 1845; " Fry's Deſcription of the Great Bible," folio, London, 1865; and " Lee's Memorial for the Bible Societies, 8vo., Edinburgh, 1824;" and Appendix, 1826. Sale Catalogues have alſo been examined, eſpecially that of the late Mr. Offor's Collection, on which, however, little dependence can be placed, as many of his bibles were wholly made up of different editions.

CONTENTS.

A Century of Bibles.

INTRODUCTORY.

HE ſtory of the Engliſh Bible has been many times written, up to a certain point. Lewis and Newcome and Strype, in the laſt century, Horne and Cotton and Tregelles in our own, have treated of it with more or leſs completeneſs within the ſcope of their reſpective deſigns: while Anderſon and Weſtcott have each in his department left little more to be recorded. But all theſe writers have ſtopped ſhort when their narrative reached the com-pletion of the verſion of 1611. Archdeacon Cotton, it is true, mentions a few editions here and there which were printed after that date,

B

but his lift only profeffes to notice thofe which were remarkable for fome fpecial reafon. The catalogue of his own collection privately printed for Mr. Lea Wilfon contains but few examples of the laft verfion in comparifon with his extenfive lift of the older Bibles. An American gentleman, Mr. Lenox, has printed fome remarks on the early editions in his library; but Mr. Fry is the firft who has collated any large number of copies of King James's Bible. This indefatigable bibliographer has fucceeded in eftablifhing the diftinctnefs of the firft folios of 1611 and their fucceffors up to 1640. After a long feries of patient refearches he has provided us with at leaft a ground-work from which any future hiftorian may continue to build, but in confining his obfervations to the folios he is obliged to leave untold the more interefting half of the ftory. It muft by no means be fuppofed that, becaufe all our bibliographers have thus left a large part of the narrative untouched, or have at moft only ftepped acrofs the boundary line previoufly fixed at 1611, nothing of intereft remains be-

yond. On the contrary, whether we regard
the further hiſtory of the Authoriſed Verſion
from a purely bibliographical point of view,
or chooſe a more general and hiſtorical aſpect
in which to examine it, we ſhall find much of
importance and more that is rather amuſing
than actually weighty : and in tracing the
various changes and chances by which the
modern Bible has been made to differ from the
original we ſhall find that it by no means
partakes of the felicity of the nation whoſe
hiſtory is a blank. Many a battle has been
fought, many a defeat ſuſtained ; many a vic-
tory has been gained for the truth. Injuries
have been inflicted by partial friends ; wounds
have been received from unſcrupulous enemies.
Although it remains ſubſtantially the ſame as
when it left the hands of the tranſlators, yet
Puritans and Calviniſts, Churchmen and Metho-
diſts, Hebraiſts and Græciſts have all left their
marks upon it. It would be too much to ſay
that the gulf which ſeparates the laſt edition
of Bagſter from the firſt of Barker, equals that
by which the Authoriſed Verſion differs from

the tentative efforts of Tyndale and Coverdale, but it is no exaggeration to aſſert that our modern Bible is altered throughout from its original, for the better in ſome places, for the worſe in ſome; and that while the general correctneſs of the printing is greater as a rule in our day, the ſpelling and punctuation might yet with advantage follow the earlier model. Theſe things appear at firſt ſight of trifling moment, yet it is with ſuch trifles that reviſers have to deal: and it is by a number of ſuch ſmall matters that the authority of the whole is moſt often teſted.

Mr. Weſtcott has detailed the external and internal hiſtory of King James's tranſlation, up to the moment at which it was launched into the world, with all its imperfections on its head. Unfortunately, as we ſhall ſee, they were many; but at this point Mr. Weſtcott breaks off. Yet the very firſt dip into the new volume brings up ſomething worth noting. The firſt title is an engraving—and a very fine one,—but the New Teſtament title is within a woodcut border: and it has a peculiarity

which at once attracts attention, a peculiarity
which it fhares with the firft title of later
iffues, alfo in woodcut.   There is no line
" *Appointed to be read in Churches.*"   Nor
does this important feature occur anywhere in
the firft octavo, the firft Teftament, the firft
quarto Teftament, the fecond quarto Bible,
the firft Roman letter folio or a great many
other editions, being, in fact, for the firft year
or fo confined to the engraved titles of two
Bibles.   This fact is an additional and valu-
able proof, although apparently unknown to
Mr. Weftcott, that he is right in faying the
prefent verfion was never in reality feparately
fanctioned by council, convocation or parliament.   In the ftrict fenfe of the word the only
verfion ever *authorifed* was the Great Bible
referred to fpecially in a proclamation of
Henry VIII., dated in 1538.   And the authority of the Bifhops' Bible depended mainly
on its being regarded as merely a revifion
of the Great Bible.   The authority of King
James's verfion in like manner may be held to
depend on its affumption of the place pre-

vioufly occupied by the Bifhops'. That in
truth this was the intention of thofe in power
is proved by the fact that no edition of the
Bifhops' Bible was afterwards iffued: and
further that the very type, head-pieces, and
even woodcuts of the Elizabethan verfion were
employed on the new edition. Thus the
figure of Neptune, which in the largeft of the
Bifhops' was made frequently available, now
headed the gofpel of St. Matthew: and fimilar
economy of material may be traced in other
places, as in the initials of the Pfalms where we
ftill fee the creft and the arms of Walfingham
and of Cecil. The fame arrangements are
traceable in the fmaller editions. The popular
Bible during the Elizabethan era had been the
Genevan: many editions of it were publifhed
both before and after the appearance of King
James's: it was almoft always in a quarto
fize and the more the new verfion could be
made to refemble the older one in its external
features, the fooner it was likely to obtain with
private readers. So we find the earlieft
quartos were affimilated as much as poffible

to the later Genevans. The Breeches Bible
of 1611 is exactly, in fize, form, and type, the
fame as the Authorifed Edition of 1613. The
title page, in particular, of 1613, is printed
with the border already fo often ufed for the
Genevan. In 1612 a handfome copperplate,
a reduction from the engraved title of the folio,
had been ufed, but only for the one iffue.
All but one of Barker's quartos—moft of them
in black letter—were iffued under the Genevan
title-page woodcut, with arms of the twelve
tribes and figures of the apoftles and evangelifts :
and at length it got fo worn and battered that
in the laft copies, printed before the Rebellion,
its minor features are barely diftinguifhable.
It is the fame, too, with the octavo editions
and the Teftaments. A block, which was in
vogue under Elizabeth for prayer books, was
now ufed for Bibles, the queen's arms being
fometimes cut out at the top and the king's
fubftituted.

The new verfion was thus fpeedily dif-
feminated in all fizes. There was no delay to
prepare frefh plant. Everything already in

ufe was made available and though the Genevan
was occafionally reprinted even as late as 1644,
the Bifhops' Teftament only occafionally re-
appears, and the complete Bible never, the new
tranflation in folio reprefenting the one, and
in quarto the other. Above fifty different
editions were printed by Barker and his fucceffors before 1638 : befides ten at Cambridge
and two at Edinburgh. No Bibles feem to
have been produced at Oxford before 1673,
although the patent for printing at the univerfity prefs dates from 1632. But of Oxford
Bibles we fhall have occafion to fpeak again
prefently.

Before going further let us endeavour to
anfwer diftinctly the queftion how far are we
juftified in calling this the " Authorifed Verfion."   Are we right or wrong in ufing the
term ?   Mr. Lea Wilfon cautioufly refers to
King James's as the " Royal Verfion," but if
we accept it, on the grounds already ftated, as
the legitimate defcendant and fucceffor of the
" Great Bible," which undoubtedly was authorifed, we fhall be content to ufe the ordinary

term. We have other facts in our favour in fo
doing. When at the Prayer Book revifion of
1662 the Epiftles and Gofpels and the fen-
tences in the morning and evening fervices
were taken from the Bible of King James,
and when the revifed prayer book was annexed
to the Act of Uniformity, a certain fanction
was given to it: a fanction which placed it on
an equal footing with the Great Bible, from
which the Pfalms and certain other parts of the
fervice are ftill taken. The note in the margin
of the corrected Book of Common Prayer
runs thus:—" *The Ep^ln & Gofpels are all to
be corrected after the laft tranflation,*" and fo
ftrictly is this injunction carried out that wher-
ever the firft editions were in error the error
is perpetuated: and to this day we read in the
Epiftle for the firft Sunday after Eafter, 1 John
v. 12, " He that hath the Son hath life, and
he that hath not the Son hath not life;" although two important words are thus omitted;
words which have fince been reftored to our
Bibles but not to our prayer books. The fame
is to be faid regarding the ufe of the word

" fometime " in the fenfe of " once ; " the
1611 Bibles giving it as " fometimes " and the
Book of Common Prayer, together with all
later Bibles, fo far as our knowledge extends,
except one by Hayes, 1673, perpetuate an
error, which did not occur in the Genevan or
the Bifhops' Verfions.

Strange to fay we have little or no contemporary evidence as to the reception accorded
to the new Bible, or as to the hiftory of the
early editions. Much however may be in-
directly gathered from the editions themfelves,
their number, their comparative rarity, and the
other points on which the labours of modern
bibliographers have been beftowed. Thefe
labours have refulted in the difcovery of many
particulars long hidden within the volumes
themfelves. Mr. Lea Wilfon probably died
in the belief that one folio only was printed in
1611. Mr. Fry has demonftrated that two
at leaft were iffued and perhaps part of a third.
His conclufions were at one time queftioned,
but without fufficient reafon : he feems to have
clearly diftinguifhed between thefe early iffues

and to have identified the firſt of them. The queſtion is really of importance. It is very deſirable that, even now, we ſhould know what was the actual deſign of the tranſlators in the ſmaller as well as in the greater particulars: for although the Phariſees were reproved for ſtraining out a gnat and ſwallowing a camel, it by no means follows that the gnat ſhould be left. To go no further than this very text (St. Matt. xxiii. 24) it is high time that the old reading ſhould be reſtored. " Strain out" occurs in the Biſhops' and Genevan verſions : " Strain at," an evident typographical error, has, with one exception, been printed in all the Royal Bibles.

The Barker family, to whom the printing of the new verſion was from the firſt committed, had long held the office of Royal Printers, by patent from Queen Elizabeth. Full details of their connection with the work will be found in Anderſon's *Annals of the Engliſh Bible*, vol. ii., *paſſim*. During the civil war we find " a companie of Stationers" uſing their type and woodcut borders, and producing in 1648 and

1649, Bibles clofely refembling theirs. An interefting paper in *Notes and Queries*, (4 S. viii.) informs us that Barker received in King James's time 6*l*. 13*s*. 4*d*. only as his annual falary, but the profits of his office muft have been very large, and he had a grant from the king of the manor of Upton in the neighbourhood of Windfor. The favour of Cecil and Walfingham was acknowledged in many ways by the Barkers. Their fhop in Paternofter Row bore the fign of the " Tyger's head," Walfingham's creft, which, with the arms of Cecil, occurs in feveral places in the woodcut initials of the Bible. In 1616 Robert Barker's fon, another Robert, obtained the extenfion to himfelf of his father's patent : and in 1627 had leave to transfer or leafe his intereft in it to Bonham Norton and John Bill. In 1635 Charles and Matthew Barker were included in the patent. In 1645 Robert the elder died, in the King's Bench. Owing to his difficulties and the many dif-turbing caufes of the Rebellion a number of other names now begin to appear on the title-pages of Bibles, but Oliver Cromwell, having

had frequent reafon to complain of the carelefs-
nefs of the Bible printers, granted a patent to
one of the moft carelefs, John Field printer to
the Univerfity of Cambridge. Befides the
Bibles of this period printed in England, a
large number were imported from Holland,
and many of the foreigners were worthy to rank
with Field in bad paper, bad type and general
incorrectnefs.

The Univerfities had early claimed the right
of printing on their own account, and Bibles
were iffued from the Cambridge prefs in 1629;
a New Teftament, poffibly, the year before.
Thefe early productions of Cambridge bear
the names of Thomas and John Buck, printers
to the Univerfity ; and are chiefly remarkable
for a mifprint in 1 Timothy iv. 16, which
originated with them, and which was continued
in all, or nearly all their Bibles, and was imitated
by other printers until the beginning of this
century, examples occurring as late as 1803.
Another and ftill more ferious error alfo takes
its rife in the Cambridge Bibles. In 1638
the corrupt ftate of the text as to the ufe of

italics, the fpelling and the punctuation, having
attracted univerfal attention, Dr. Ward, and
Dr. Goad, with other divines, fuperintended
the publication of a folio edition in which
undoubtedly they made many corrections, but
alfo allowed the mifreading in 1 Timothy iv. 16,
and added a reading, in Acts vi. 3, which was
afterwards ufed by the Independents againft
the epifcopal party; fo much fo, indeed, that
the corruption itfelf is often attributed to them.
It is undoubted that this reading was in favour
with the Puritans, and we find it in almoft all
their Bibles: it confifted in the alteration of a
fingle letter, by which the apoftles are made
to commit the ordination of deacons to the
congregation: " Look ye out among you
feven men of honeft report . . . whom *ye* may
appoint over this bufinefs." The pronoun
fhould have been " we." This folio of 1638,
bears the names of Thomas Buck and Roger
Daniel, printers to the Univerfity. Soon after,
John Field appears in the fame capacity, and
his Bibles are iffued alfo, in accordance with
the Protector's patent, from a London prefs.

At the Reftoration his further operations were confined to Cambridge where he continued to hold his office until 1670, after which date the name of John Hayes is fubftituted.

But Scotland was at leaft as early in the field as Cambridge.   In 1628 the " heirs of Andrew Hart," who had printed Genevan Bibles eighteen years before, iffued a New Teftament, and in 1633 a Bible in fpecial celebration, it is faid, of the coronation of Charles at Scone.   Be this as it may, confiderable ftir was created by the illuftrations introduced, fome faid by Laud, into the new Bible, and many were the epithets heaped upon the " Popifh pictures" by the fucceffors of Knox. In 1670 a New Teftament was printed at Glafgow, and not until 1675 was the firft Oxford Bible iffued.   The colophon of this Bible is dated two years earlier but the New Teftament does not feem to have been publifhed alone.   A large number of the productions of the Oxford prefs followed in the enfuing years. They all bear the imprint, " at the Theater " and were ufually commiffioned by London

bookfellers. Among thefe appear moft often
the names of Ann Leake, a widow, carrying
on bufinefs in Fetter Lane, Fleet Street, and
Thomas Guy of Lombard Street, who afterwards became the munificent founder of the
Hofpital which bears his name. Meanwhile
the production of Bibles at Cambridge had
waned, and the London printers, although
their patent continued until the firft years of
the eighteenth century, were by no means as
prolific as the Oxford " Theater." Moft of
the London Bibles of this period bear the
names fucceffively of John Bill and Chriftopher
Barker, or of their affigns ; of Bill, Newcomb
and Hills ; and of Charles Bill and the executrix of Thomas Newcomb : but many with
notes were alfo printed by other firms ; the
notes being fometimes only inferted to evade
the patent, and being printed low down at the
foot of the page to be cut off by the binder.
The moft common of thefe productions was
publifhed by Pafham in 1776 and is fomewhat
fcarce in an unmutilated form : but as this
edition dates later than the period to which

our lift relates it will not be neceffary to purfue the fubject.

During the whole of this period a furreptitious importation had come from Holland. The competition was fometimes very fierce and as the foreign editions were generally remarkable for errors and omiffions a practice fprung up of dating them as if they were the production of the London firms, nor was this fraud unknown within the kingdom. Several examples have been accidentally recognized in Scottifh Bibles and are diftinguifhed by bibliographers. But the moft remarkable foreign examples are two duodecimos; one of them dated 1638, but in reality printed at Amfterdam many years later, full of abfurd mifprints, fuch as, " fons of Belial" for " fons of Bilhah," " fhamefulnefs" for " fhamefacednefs" and many more : and the other, dated 1684, which is betrayed by the miffpelling of a word on the title-page, "the Affings" of Bill and Barker. Other Dutch Bibles again were publifhed anonymoufly, fome with a view of London on the title-page, and others, and

c

thefe generally with Genevan notes, with the
initials of John Canne or fome other Amfterdam
printer.   A large number were produced by
Steven Swart, in the fame city, and fubfequently
by his widow.   It is alfo ufual to attribute to
the foreign prefs an Edinburgh blackletter
Teftament dated in 1694, which may be confidered on the whole entitled to the difgraceful
diftinction of having diftanced all competitors
in carelefs and erroneous typography.   It
may fafely be afferted that a miftake occurs in
every column; hardly a verfe is without one
at leaft, and Dr. Lee eftimates the whole
number at 2,000.   Thus in S. Mark vii. 35,
we read of the deaf mute "and ftraightway
his *eyes* were opened . . . and he fpake plain;"
and in S. Luke, ii. 36 that Anna "had lived
with an hufband *feventy* years."   A Glafgow
Teftament of 1691 is nearly as bad.

Whilft we are on the fubject we may here
enumerate the other editions remarkable for
mifprints, or, as in fome cafes for general incorrectnefs. At the head of thefe ftands Barker's
octavo of 1631.   It abounds in grofs errors,

of which one example will fuffice. In the
commandments as given at Exodus xx, the
important word " not " is omitted in the
fourteenth verfe, which therefore reads, " Thou
fhalt commit adultery." It has often been
afferted that Barker " and Lucas" the King's
printers were fummoned before the Star Cham-
ber and fined 3,000*l.* for this careleffnefs : but
no one of the name of Lucas is known to
have held any fuch office and the fum paid by
Barker dwindles on inveftigation to 300*l.* ; and
even this again is compounded for by the pre-
fentation of a fet of Greek types to one of
the Univerfities. Miftakes of flighter importance will be frequently found in the enfuing
lift. Among thefe are fuch examples as " fonne "
for " name," S. Matt. i. 25 ; " the queen of
the South fhall up in the Judgment with this
generation," S. Matt. xii. 42, both in a Cambridge quarto of 1637. The Tranflators are
called the " Trancelators" in a black-letter
quarto of 1619-20, and II Corinthians is called
II *Coain*thians. This epiftle is fingularly unfortunate in the annals of errata, for in the

second folio, issued in 1611, in which the mis-
takes committed in the first were supposed to
be corrected, we find First and Second Corinthians substituted in the List of Books for
First and Second Chronicles. The same volume
contains an even more serious error: in Matt.
xxvi. 36, we read, " Then commeth *Judas*
with them unto a place called Gethsemane;"
while in many copies the right name, printed
on a slip is pasted over. The first folio itself
had many errors but never aught like this:
the most important being a repetition of three
lines in Exodus xiv. 10, and the number
" eleven thousand" for " thirteen hundred
thousand" in the heading of II Samuel xxiv.
The folio of 1613 is extremely incorrect, but
the period of the Commonwealth was most
remarkable as we have seen for the corruption
of the printed text, although very few examples
are worth quoting, the faults being more of
general carelessness than of actual misprinting.
Some cases, however, are notorious. Thus,
in one or more of Field's Bibles, 1658, 24mo.
" As the chief is ashamed when he is found,"

fhould be " As the thief is afhamed :" and in
a Cambridge 8vo. of 1657 a large part of the
4th verfe of Pfalm cxliii is omitted.   Kilburne
mentions ninety-one faults in another of Field's,
12mo. 1655 : and the quarto with notes printed
in 1649 has many mifprints, one or two of
them very important.   The general incorrectnefs of Bible printing is by no means confined
to thofe times of difturbance.   The Errata of
Field's little volumes are emulated in Blayney's
folio of 1769, (Oxford, Wright and Gill,)
which abounds in omiffions and mifprints : yet
this is ftill confidered a ftandard edition.   Many
of Bagfter's Bibles contain ferious errors, and
even the Bible Society has not been exempt
from the failings of which we complain.   An
octavo printed at Cambridge in 1831 reads
Pfalm cxix. 93, " I will never forgive thy precepts," and 1 John iii. 11. " love another," *for*
" love one another."   An Oxford 8vo. of
1792 names St. Philip inftead of St. Peter in
St. Luke xxii. 34.   Bafkett's fine folio of
1717 is known as the *vinegar Bible* from the
mifprint in the heading of the parable of the

vineyard in the fame chapter : and an 8vo. of
1711 omits the "not" in the laft claufe of
Ifaiah lvii. 12.   Dr. Lee gives many examples
in his *Memorial.*   Thus in an Edinburgh quarto
of 1791, he found, "Make me not to go in
the way of thy commandments" Pfalm cxix.
33 : in a New Teftament, 1816, "let all
tongues be done decently ;" in two quartos,
1811 and 1814, "the blaft of the terrible ones
is as a *ftone* againft the wall :" whilft he fays
"it might difturb the gravity even of well
difpofed perfons to hear," at 1 Kings xxii. 38,
"the dogs *liked* his blood" in another Scottifh
Bible of 1791.   The number of examples in
Dr. Lee is very great, and leave an unpleafant
impreffion of the Edinburgh Editions, but we
have no caufe to congratulate ourfelves on any
immunity in the Southern part of our ifland.
In a Cambridge 12mo. of 1828, Mr. Curtis
found thefe among other errors :—S. Matt.
xxii. 28, whofe wife fhall fhe be, *for* whofe
wife : and Heb. xiii. 2, bet not, *for* be not :
and in an 18mo., by Reeves, "his own wife
alfo, *for* his own life.   This word, *wife,* is par-

ticularly unfortunate for in one of the Bibles
12mo, 1638, defcribed in our lift, the heathen
are fpoken of as vexing the Ifraelites with their
" wives," (for " wiles ") in Numbers xxv. 18.

Befides fuch aberrations as thefe there is a
large clafs of various readings which will
require notice more at length. Some of them,
owing to the prefent endeavour to amend the
text, are of fpecial intereft. Others, of fmaller
moment in themfelves are remarkable as examples of the mifchief which may be occafioned by a fingle carelefs compofitor, while
many, into the merits of which we will not
enter here, are concerned with the ufe of italics,
the fpelling of proper names, the punctuation,
and what may be confidered to belong to the
more purely critical departments of Biblical
refearch.

Printers and correctors of the prefs have at
all times taken upon themfelves without any
fpecial authority to amend the text in minor
matters, fuch as fpelling. The fpelling of no
two editions during the firft century will be
found exactly alike. Even in the fame verfe

the fame word is fpelled in different ways, fometimes, as in the firft verfe of Deut. xxix, in three: and fometimes a Bible will be met with in which, as in Field's 12mo, of 1657, the fpelling approximates nearly to that of our modern editions; while, years later, the old fpelling will be found in another edition. We ftill have fuch words as *plow*, *aftonied*, *throughly*, *pranfings*, *fope*; although the authority by which they are retained has no more exiftence in reality than that by which fuch words as *fhamefaftnefs* or *unpoffible* were altered. Two or three examples of modern alterations and infertions are worth noticing. They are fe-lected as they come to hand:—

In the firft folio and in all later editions until 1630, at leaft, we read in Romans xii. 2, " that good, *that* acceptable and perfect will of God." It would be difficult to find a reafon for the change now univerfal, of the fecond *that* into *and*.

In the firft folio and moft fubfequent editions until the prefent century we read in St. Matt. xii. 23, " Is this the Son of David?" Dr.

Blayney inſerted a " not," in 1769. The change is an improvement, but what was his authority for making it? The old reading occurs laſt in a 4to., Cambridge 1837.

In the firſt folio we read, 1 John v. 12, " He that hath not the Son hath not life." In 1638 this was altered to our preſent reading which inſerts " of God " after ſon : but the old reading remains, as we have already ſeen, in our prayer books.

Again, we have two erroneous readings re-tained neither of which occurs in the previous verſions. In Epheſians, ii. 13, and other places we have already ſeen that " ſometimes " is printed for " ſometime," a word of wholly dif-ferent meaning. Again, as we have mentioned above, the Genevan Bibles had in S. Matt. xxiii. 24, " ſtrain *out* a gnat," but this reading which is very probably right never occurs in any edition of the Authoriſed Verſion, before 1754 : nor ever ſince, ſo far as we are aware. The ſame printer who in 1769 changed " world " into " earth " at 1 Cor. iv. 13, and inſerted the important word " Godly " before " edifying "

in 1 Tim. i. 4, might furely have given a
corrected reading of thefe paffages.

But a ftill more curious field for inveftigation is prefented by the viciffitudes of head
lines, and headings. Thefe have been altered
and reftored over and over again. The tender
fufceptibilities of the Puritan were often as
much wounded by the high church headings
as thofe of the followers of Laud by the Genevan notes. Some of the Bibles of the commonwealth omit the headings: in others their
meaning is modified to fuit the times. The
moft important example is prefented by the
contents of Pfalm cxlix. " *The prophet exhorteth to praife God for his love to the church,
and for that power which he hath given to the
church to rule the confciences of men.*" So we
have it in the firft folio and in all other editions
before 1649. But in a quarto of that year,
printed by a company of Stationers and fur-
nifhed with the Genevan notes, we have this
heading thus: — " *The prophet exhorteth to
praife God for his love to the church, and for that
power which he hath given to the church, for the*

converſion of ſinners."   And in the larger number of ſubſequent Bibles the heading breaks off
cautiouſly at the firſt uſe of the word church."
" *The prophet exhorteth to praiſe God for his
love to the Church."*   In 1660 we find the
older reading reſtored in Field's 4to (the
preaching Bible :) and it underwent yet another
change a little later : for in 1769 (Blayney,) we
find " *and for that power which he hath given
to his ſaints."*   Nor is this the end : for in
modern Bibles, the repetition of the word
" Church " is reſtored, although the debateable
matter at the end of the original headings is
omitted.   In Bagſter's Polyglots ſuch queſtions are avoided by the total omiſſion of all
headings.

Further we need not go in this place.   The
queſtions, and they are many and difficult,
which relate to the uſe of italics will be found
well treated of by Dr. Turton, in *The Text of the
Engliſh Bible, conſidered. (Second Edition, Oxford,* 1833).   Almoſt all the critical queſtions
will be found briefly ſtated by Mr. Girdleſtone
of the Bible Society, in a paper by him in the

Chriſtian Advocate, April 1870, whilſt the differences by which the preſent authoriſed verſion is diſtinguiſhed from its predeceſſors will be ſeen at conſiderable length in Mr. Weſtcott's *Hiſtory of the Engliſh Bible.* Many other works might be named, ſuch as Mr. Blunt's *Plain Account,* and Archdeacon Cotton's *Editions of the Bible* in which much information will be found, but none of theſe, and indeed, no work with which we are acquainted gives the hiſtory of our preſent verſion beyond the date at which it was publiſhed.

It is perhaps too much to hope that a future volume may be devoted to the editions publiſhed ſince 1711. Had it been poſſible a liſt of the editions of the Pſalms and of parts of the Bible ſhould have been included: but in theſe particulars Dr. Cotton's work is very full, and a new liſt would have only been a réchauffé from his, without freſh facts, and perhaps without any additions. Dr. Lee's *Memorial for the Bible Societies in Scotland,* with two Appendices, 1824-6, has been largely drawn upon. The liſts of Scottiſh Bibles will be found very deficient, as no materials exift from which any detailed account may be derived.

The Bibles and Teftaments enumerated below have as far as poffible been perfonally examined. The larger part are to be found in the Britifh Mufeum. Where that noble collection failed to fhow an edition, Mr. Francis Fry of Briftol, Mr. Euing of Glafgow, and Mr. T. M. Ward of Maida Hill have afforded the kindeft and moft neceffary information. Of the other collections which have been ranfacked perhaps the moft important is that of the Venerable B. Harrifon, Archdeacon of Maidftone, which is at prefent depofited in the Cathedral Library at Canterbury ; it contains what is probably a unique feries of the Oxford Bibles publifhed by Thomas Guy. Many examples which are named in Sale Catalogues are not to be found. In fuch cafes the catalogue in which the miffing volume is named will be mentioned, unlefs good reafons exift for fuf-pecting that a miftake has been made. It will alfo be feen that in feveral places Mr. Lea Wilfon's eftimate of the fize has been departed from.   This is only done when the fignatures are fufficiently orderly to allow of an accurate eftimate.   In other cafes, editions named by him will be found differently entered: this is becaufe he gave but one date, the firft, and it is not therefore fometimes poffible to diftinguifh the edition intended.   In cafes of mixed dates that of the Old Teftament or general title is allowed to prevail, and if the New Teftament is of earlier date the Bible will be claffed before the others of the fame (general) date.   All the productions of the London prefs are enumerated firft under each year: the Cambridge Bibles, if any follow next, after them the Oxford, if any, then thofe printed in Scotland and laft, foreign productions.   In each cafe the New Teftaments follow the editions of the complete Bible.

The Bibles of the Authorifed Verfion enumerated in the Britifh Mufeum Catalogue will be found in a feparate lift, the fizes being given as they are there written: and the Bibles and Teftaments in Mr. Lea Wilfon's Catalogue are alfo briefly tabulated, with one or two other fhort lifts which may be found ufeful.

In order to render this volume more useful to the bibliographer Kilburne's Tract, which is often alluded to throughout the work, is here reprinted entire from the copy in the Britifh Mufeum (1214. a. 9). It is a fmall 4to or 8vo. The Title:—" Dangerous Errors in Several late printed Bibles: To the great fcandal and corruption of found and true Religion. Difcovered by William Kilburne, Gent.

Ex parva fcintilla magnum incendium.
Principiis obfta, fero medicina paratur
Cum mala per longas invaluere moras.

Printed at Finfbury, Anno 1659.

An animadverfion to all good Chriftians of this Commonwealth, difcovering (amongft many Thoufands of others) fome pernicious erroneous & corrupt Erratas Efcapes & Faults in feveral Impreffions of the Holy Bible *and* Teftament, *within thefe late years, commonly vended & difperfed to the great fcandal of Religion but more particularly in the Impreffions of* Henry Hills *&* John Field, *printers; To the intent that either in reading of any fuch already bought or buying the like hereafter, they may be well advifed, for the good of their own fouls & the generations that fhall fucceed.*

Publifhed by *William Kilburne*, Gent.

(*Honourable and elect Christians.*

The sacred Scriptures are the Crystalline
Fountain, from whence all the lucid streams
and Rivulets of pure Religion are derived and
conducted into the Cisterns and Receptacles of
the hearts and understandings of Christians;
whereby they may be directed, and instructed
to lead a gracious and holy life here and pre-
pared for, & assured of a glorious and eternal
life hereafter: And what accurate diligence
venerable respect the antient Jews, did use,
and bear towards the *Pentateuch,* & other
Divine Books of Canonical Scripture of the
old Testament, in accounting the number of
words Syllables, nay Letters thereof : And also
the sedulity of Christians since the death of
Christ (through all the terrible and Sanguineous
persecutions of cruel Tyrants) to convey from
age to age the Testament of our blessed Saviour,
and Writings and Epistles of his Holy
Apostles in their purity, (whereby they have
been by God's providence preserved from
corruption) should incite, and invite *us* (who
have received a greater Illumination, and Re-

formation, than the Iews or primitive Christians,) carefully to promulge and propagate the
word of God in its intrinsical virtue, and propriety; Considering the many Heresies and
false Doctrines professed in our days; And
that it was the Arch-policy and designe of
the Devil in tempting our very Saviour (as
Math. 4. 6. and *Luke* 4. 10, 11. compared
with *Psal*. 91. 11, 12.) to pervert, and falsely
produce the authority & parallel of the Scripture: And when as also in the Primitive
times one ἰῶτα, (the least Letter of the Alpha-
bet) occasioned so great a controversie in God's
Church, under the Empire of *Constantine* the
Great. For in the Doctrine of the everblessed
Trinity, in the debates of the *Nicene Councel*,
Athenasius, and the *Orthodox* party held, that
Christ was Ὁμοούσιος, and of the same Essence
of God his Father; the *Arrians*, and Hetero-
dox, Ὁμοιούσιος, making him a meer Creature,
and depriving him of his royal Diadem of the
eternall Divinity; Which two words differ
but in one Letter. And we read *Iudges* 12.
6. that the *Gileadites* slew of the *Ephraimites*

42,000 fouls for not pronouncing rightly *Shibboleth*, and miffing but in one Afpiration.

You may well remember that the zeal and care of the late Bifhops (efpecially of reverend and learned Doctor Ufher) was fuch, that for the omiffion in one impreffion of the Bible of the *Negative* word [*Not*] in the feventh Commandment, the Printer was fined 2000 or 3000*l.* in the late King's time, as I have heard, which hapned long before the late wars began : In which time through the abfence of the King's Printers, and ceffation of Bible Printing at *London*, many erroneous Englifh Bibles were printed in, and imported from *Holland;* which, being diligently compared by the late *Affembly of Divines*, were reported to the *Parliament* in 1643 to be corrupt, and dangerous to Religion ; exhibiting to them thefe three faults only ; for which the impreffion was fuppreffed and condemned to the fire, and a Prohibition made againft the Importation of any Englifh Bibles for the future. viz.

Gen. 36. 24. *This is that Ana that found Rulers in the wildernefs* .... for *mules.*

Ruth 4. 13. *The Lord gave her Corruption
. . . . for Conception.*

Luke 21. 28. *Look up and lift up your
heads for your Condemnation draweth nigh . . . .
for Redemption.*

This Affair alfo occafioned the faid Affembly by direction of the Parliament (as is very
well known to Mr. *Philip Nye*) &c. to propofe
the Bible printing to feveral Stationers of *London ;* who refufing that laudable work, the fame
was commended to Mr. *William Bentley* Printer
in *Finfbury*, and his partners, who have fo exactly, and commendably imprinted feveral volumes by Authority of Parliament in 8°. and 12°.
in the years 1646. 48. 51, &c. (according to
the authentique corrected *Cambridge Bible*, revifed *Mandato Regio*, by the learned Doctor
Ward, Doctor *Goad* of *Hadley*, M^r. Boyfe,
M^r. Mead, &c. and printed by the elaborate
induftry of *Thomas Buck* Efquire and M^r.
Roger Daniel in *folio* in 1638,) that fome fmall
remainders of them yet unfold are now daily
expofed at 12*s. per* Book in quires unbound by
the Stationers (for the fairnefs of the Print,
and truth of the Editions) which Mr. *Bentley*

afforded heretofore at 2*s*. *per* Book, or there-
abouts, untill he hath been unjuſtly obſtructed
by Mr. *Hills* and Mr. *Field*, who have endeavoured, by abuſing the Authority of the
State to *Monopolize* the ſole printing of Bibles
to themſelves ſince the latter end of the year
1655, and have raiſed the prizes to exceſſive
dear rates, to the very great ſcandal of Religion,
and detriment of the Commonwealth : For-
aſmuch as they have printed and diſperſed in
theſe late years divers Editions in ſeveral
volumes under their ſeveral Names and Titles,
that if you be pleaſed to compare and examine
the ſame, you will find amongſt many great
numbers of others, verbal, literal, and in the
points of diſtinction theſe groſs and notorious
Erratas, Eſcapes, and Faults following ; which
I recommend to your ingenuous conſideration
and benevolent conſtruction having heretofore
repreſented ſome of them to his late Highneſs,
and the moſt of them to the late Parliament.

   1. In a Pearl Bible printed by *John Field* at
London in 1653. in volume 24°. (very ſmall
to carry in pockets) whereof there have been

neer 20000 difperfed, are thefe egregious faults, viz. :—

All the Dedications and Titles of *David's* Pfalms are wholly left out, being part of the original Text in *Hebrew,* and intimating the caufe, and occafion of the writing and compofing thofe Pfalms, whereby the matter may be better illuftrated.

John 9. 21. *Or who hath opened his eyes we know not.* Thefe words are wholly omitted.

Rom. 6. 13. *Neither yield ye your members as inftruments of righteoufnefs unto fin.* for *unrighteoufnefs.*

1 *Cor.* 6. 9. *Know ye not that the unrighteous fhall inherit the Kingdom of God?* for *Shall not inherit.* This is the foundation of a damnable Doctrine for it hath been averred by a reverend Doctor of Divinity to feveral worthy perfons, that many Libertines and licentious people did produce, and urge this Text from the authority of this corrupt Bible againft his mild Reproofs, in Juftification of their vicious and inordinate Converfations.

2. In a fmall Bible in volume 12°. printed

by *John Field* at *London* in 1655. whereof great
numbers have been diſperſed.

A Catalogue of 91 notorious faults, amongſt
many others therein were preſented by Mr.
Hills to Mr. Secretary of Eſtate, and by him
recommended to an honourable Member of
the late Parliament.　One whereof is 2 Cor.
13. 6.　*But I truſt that ye ſhall know that
we are not Reprobates.* which verſe is wholly
omitted.

3. In another Bible in volume 12. printed
alſo by *John Field* at *London* in 1655. whereof
great numbers have been diſperſed.

Upon my reading of the ſix firſt Chapters
only in St. *Matthew*, I found 10. notable faults
& have received general information from per-
ſons of worth, that the reſidue of the book is
correſpondent ; which was evidenced to a Com -
mittee of Parliament, inſomuch that they ſiezed
them and prohibited the ſale thereof and of the
former Bibles in Mr. *Field's* hands, as alſo of
the enſuing Bible, which notwithſtanding that
reſtraint, he hath ſince divulged.

4. In a Bible in volume 12. printed by

John Field at *London* in 1656. you may obferve thefe faults *viz.*

Ifai. 10. 26.   Cap. 13. 3;   Cap. 14. 24. Cap. 17. 8.   Cap. 18. 17.   *And the waters fhall overthrow the hiding place.* for *overflow.*   Cap. 48. 19.   Cap. 49. 22. and fo generally through the whole old Teftament.   But in the new Teftament be pleafed to perufe thefe, *viz.*

Luk. xxiii. 42, 51.   Cap. 24. 24.   Joh. 1. 51.   Cap. 2. 9, 10.   Cap. 3. 21.   Cap. 5. 2. *the pool Bethfaida* for *Bethefda, ver.* 23.   *As they honour their Father,* for *the Father* Emphatically.   Cap. 6. 29, 33.   Cap. 7. 39.   *But this fpake he of the fpirits,* which they that believe on him fhould receive, for *fpirit,* fpeaking onely of the Holy Ghoft, as appeareth in the fame verfe.   *Cap.* 13. 22.   *Cap.* 14. 13, 21.   *And he that loveth me fhall loved* for *fhall be loved of my Father.   Cap.* 15. 17.   Thefe things I commanded, for *command you.   Cap.* 17. 12. *That the Scriptures might be fulfilled,* for *Scripture,* fpeaking of *Iudas* the fonne of perdition, and referring to *Pfal.* 109. 8.   *Cap.* 19. 37. *Cap.* 20. 25.   *And put my fingers,* for *finger.*

Cap. 21. 17. *Act.* 1. 7. *Cap.* 4. 15. *Counsel* (*or advice*) for Councell (or a confistorie). And this is often reiterated in other places. *Cap.* 8. 36. A very bafe omiffion, and falfe juftification of the words to the confufion of the fenfe. *Cap.* 13. 1, 6, 26. *he,* for *they,* a groffe fault. *Rom.* 4. 10. *Cap.* 6. 23. meer nonfenfe. 1 *Joh.* 4. 20. 2 *Joh. ver.* 1. *Rev.* 1. 1. *Cap.* 21. 10.

I might particularize many more, efpecially in the Contents ; which generally are falfely perverted, and mutilated to the great impediment, and obftruction of the right underftanding of the fcope and text of the chapters.

5. In another Minion Bible in 8°· volume, printed by *John Field* at *Cambridge* in 1657. Which fels very much, and very dear, at leaft for 8*s.* 6*d. per* book.

Pfal. 143. 4. *Therefore is my Spirit over,* is wholly omitted in many that I have feen. And there are many other faults as I am well informed of very great notoriety.

6. In a Bible in 12° volume printed at *London* by *Hen. Hills* and I. *Field* in *An.* 1656.

corrected by one Mr. *Robinson* (a *Scotch Rabbi,*) and publiſhed in an Advertiſement by *Mercurius Politicus 6 Nov.* 1656. to be incomparable. And in truth I think he was not deceived, (though indeed he abuſed the Commonwealth ;) For I am confident, if the number of the Impreſſion was as (I am informed) 20000 there are as many faults therein verbal, literal, and in the difference of the *Italique* words, (to the great corruption of the Text,) and in falſe points of diſtinction : ſo that beſides the baſe paper, and printing, and abridgement, and perverſion of the Contents, and tranſpoſing and confounding of words, whereby it is very troubleſome to be read, it is the worſt of all the reſt that are expoſed to your view ; as appeared palpably to the Parliament, whereby the ſale thereof (*ſedente Parliamento*) was inhibited, but ſince diſperſed very much at Countrey Fairs, and Markets by Bookbinders and petty Chapmen, being no fitting Book for ſale by Stationers in *London ;* wherein you may obſerve theſe faults, *viz.*

Gen. 1. 21. *Cod.* for *God.* and ſo in many

other places. Cap. 7. 3. *Cap.* 10. 19. *Cap.*
15. 3. *Abraham,* before God changed his
name, for *Abram.* Cap. 18. 1. *Cap.* 27. 45.
Cap. 34. 21. *Cap.* 46. 17. Exod. 12. 42.
Cap. 16. 19. *Cap.* 19. 24. *Cap.* 26. 8. *Cap.*
29. 22. *Cap.* 40. in the Contents. *A cloud
cloudeth* for *covereth, ver.* 2. *Lev.* 3. 6. *Sac-
rifice of* left out. *Cap.* 7. 38. *Cap.* 8. 14.
Cap. 10. 18. *Cap.* 11. 3. *Cap.* 13. 55. *Cap.*
15. 20. *Cap.* 22. 12. *Cap.* 23. 35. Numb.
1. 10. *Cap.* 6. 14. *Ram.* for *Lamb. Cap.*
10. 29. *Cap.* 17. in the Contents *Kept* for
Left. Cap. 20. 12. *Cap.* 23. 15. *Cap.* 24.
12. *Cap.* 30. in the Contents *Delivered* for
Divorced. Cap. 31. 30. *Sheep* for *Flocks
Cap.* 34. 9. *Out* for *On. Deut.* 5. 29. *Cap.*
29. 5. *waked* for *waxen. Cap.* 34. 7. A
groſſe fault. *Joſhu.* 3. 11. another grand one.
Cap. 23. 16. *Goods* for *Gods. Judg.* 9. 17.
And advanced his life for *adventured his life.
Cap.* 15. 10. *Samon,* for *Samſon.* 1 Sam. 24.
9. 2 Sam. 8. 12. groſſe faults. 1 *King* 20.
6, 30. the like, 2 King. 3. 2. *Cap.* 8. 5.
The *Chronicles* and *Ezra* are generally falſe in

the proper Names. *Nehem.* 8. 17. *Had the Children of Israel done so* for *Had not.* *Esther,* 4. 1. a grosse fault. *Job* 4. 6. *Is not this thy fear, thy confidence, the uprightness of thy ways, and thy hope?* for *Is not thy fear, thy confidence and the uprightness of thy ways, thy hope?* The Titles of divers Psalms are falsely named. *Prov.* 29. 13. *Yea, he shall give delight thy soul,* for *unto thy soul.* *Eccles.* 1. 1. *Cap.* 8. 17. *Yet he shall not find it,* is wholly left out. In the Prophets are great numbers of verbal faults, and omissions, which I pretermit. In the Evangelists are many egregious faults, *viz.*

Luk. 6. 22. *Cap.* 7. 43. A base squabble and nonsense. *Cap.* 9. 13. *Loves* for *Loaves.* *Cap.* 16. 17. *Title of the Law* for *Tittle.* *Cap.* 19. 44. *Ioh.* 3. 17. *For God sent not his* Sou *into the world,* for *Sonne, ver.* 21. *Cap.* 6. 11. *Loves* for *Loaves.* *Cap.* 18. 9, 36. Grosse faults, and a dangerous corruption *viz. If my Kingdome were of this Word* for *World.* *Acts* 2. 27. *Because thou wilt not leave my* Oul *in Hell,* for *Soul,* &c. *Cap.* 9. 36. *Cap.*

10. 14. *Cap.* 21. 2. Nonſenſe. *Cap.* 24. 24.
Jew for *Jeweſſes*. *Cap.* 26. 2. Nonſenſe.
Rom. 1. 7. *Cap.* 9. 23. *Cap.* 11. 14, 32.
A groſſe error, *viz. Concluded all in unbelief*
for *them all*, to wit, the Jews. 1 *Cor.* 1. 2, 14.
Cap. 3. 15. *Cap.* 9. 22. *men* for *means.*
2 *Cor.* 8. 9. *Cap.* 11. 32. *Of the Damaſcens,*
left out. 2 *Theſ.* 2. 16. *Heb.* 9. 8, 15. *Cap.*
12. 1. 1 *Pet.* 2. Nonſenſe in the Contents.
Exhorteth for *Dehorteth,* ver. 21. *Leaving* us
as *an example.* A dangerous Error. 2 *Pet.*
1. 11, 19. 1 *Joh.* 2. 24. *Cap.* 4. 10. *Jud.*
ver. 4. *Rev.* 9. 18. *Cap.* 17. 4, 14. *Cap.*
19. 10. *Cap.* 22. 17.

7. Moreover during the time of the late
Parliament, great numbers of Bibles in a large
12° volume, were imported from *Holland* in
1656 with this falſe Title (*Imprinted at* London
by Rob. Barker, &c. *Anno* 1638.) wherein Mr.
Kiffin and Mr. *Hills* cannot be excuſed, (if
reports be true,) being contrary to the ſeveral
Acts of Parliament of 20° *Sep.* 1649. and 7.
Janu, 1652. for regulating of Printing. Wherein
are ſo many notorious *Erratas,* falſe Engliſh,

Nonfenfe, and Corruptions, that in reading part of *Genefis*, I found 30 grand faults, as *Cap.* 27. 16. *Mouth of his neck*, for *Smooth of his neck*. *Cap.* 29. 13. *She* for *He ran to meet him*. *Cap.* 30. 40. *Put them unto*, for *Put them not unto Labans Cattle*. And in reading *Ecclefiaftes, Canticles*, and the firft 27. Chapters of *Ifaiah*, I found almoft an hundred groffe faults, which I did fpecifie to the *Parliament*, and therefore omit them here ; The very Importation of the Books being an offence contrary to the faid Statutes and ought defervedly to be fuppreffed ; which notwithftanding are difperfed in the Country as aforefaid.

You may alfo take notice of another fault difcovered to me by a Reverend Minifter, efcaped in a 4°. Bible of *John Field's*, printed at *London* (1648.) (amongft many other faults therein). *viz.*

Pfal. 105. 29. *He turned their waters into blood & flew their Flefh*, for *Fifh*.

And in the finging Pfalms by him printed, bound up with feveral volumes of his Bibles, amongft others, See *Pfalm* 67. 2. *That all the*

earth may know the way to worldly wealth, for
Godly wealth.

Having thus reprefented the premiffes to
your own ocular demonftration; and confider-
ing the Curfe pronounced *Rev.* xxii. *ver.* 18. 19.
and other Texts of Scripture to that purpofe:
as alfo that the pious and *Orthodox* Minifters
do generally complain againft the faid erroneous
Bibles, I fubmit the whole matter to you;
Praying God to inflame your hearts with a
fervent love of the truth, and confirm you in
the true faith of Chriftianity; And that it will
gracioufly pleafe his divine Majefty of his
infinite goodnefs, and mercy, to blefs this
Common-Wealth with the like difpenfation of
his bleffed Word in our own proper Dialect,
and fpeech as it is in the original *Idiomes,* by
the Zeal and Patronage of his *Highnefs,* and
the *Parliament;* And that for the private
Emolument of any perfons (how great foever,)
the Scriptures may not be hereafter careleffly
and erroneoufly printed, whereby to fave the
charges of good Correction, and Printing, as
may be plainly proved by fuch Bibles, which

have been printed in late years, or elfe (as is
pretended) the profit will not countervaile the
charge: For (as it is credibly reported) Mr.
Hills & Mr. *Field* have feveral times affirmed,
that they are engaged to pay 500*l. per Annum.*
to fome, whofe names out of refpeft to them I
forbear to mention, over and above 100*l. per
Annum* to Mr. *Marchamont Needham,* and his
wife, out of the profits of the fale of their
Bibles, deriding, infulting, and triumphing over
others of the Printing Myterie, out of their
confidence in their great Friends and purfe, as
it is faid, as if they lawleffe, and free (notwithftanding the truth of the premiffes and other
grand Enormities often committed by them)
both from offence and punifhment, to the great
difhonour of the Common-wealth in general,
and dammage of many private perfons in particular.

For redreffe of which inconvenience, and
for that I am informed by a Gentleman of
Eminence, that upon his own reading of one
of their late printed Bibles, he hath noted and
obferved above 6000 faults therein, I humbly

propofe (out of my unfeigned refpects to the
publique good) that the future printing of
Bibles may neither be folely appropriated to
Mr. *Hills* & Mr. *Field* on pretence of their
purchafing the tranflated coppy, made in *An.*
1611° and unduely entring it lately as their
private Copy, and for their fole propriety in
the Stationers Regifter; For that is neither
rational, nor political, that the State fhould be
devefted of the Patronage, and protection of
the word of God, tranflated into Englifh primi-
tively at their charge, and perpirtted to be
printed onely *Cum Privilegio Regali* (being the
national and common Evidence of our Religion,
and like an *Elyfian flower* of Supremacie) and
that we fhould make our defence thereof by
and under the private and perfon Title of Mr.
Hills and Mr. *Field*, and their Affigns for per-
petuity. Nor fecondly that the Bible printing
may be left again fo loofely, and irregularly
(as of late years it was and is now in defign and
project again) to the liberty of any perfons free
of the Stationers Company, or qualified to print
for that then a greater mifchief will enfue,

than at prefent, as common reafon will demon-
ftrate.   But thirdly that fuch Printers only,
as have heretofore difcharged themfelves with
the greateft care and confcience, and for the
honour, and beft accomodation and fervice of the
Common wealth either at *London* or *Cambridge*,
and have alfo had the full approbation, and
allowance of Parliament, in and for printing of
Bibles, and fuch others as fhall be thought meet
(not exceeding in the whole, fome competent
number of able Mafter printers) may be hereafter authorifed, and permitted to print the
Bible under the States privilege only, and not
as their own private Copy, under fuch qualifi-
cations, and provifions for good Correction
Workmanfhip, and price, as fhal be expedient
for the better ordering and accomplifhing of
fuch an honourable, laudable, and weighty
work and employment.

"London, 1° Januarij 1659 Stylo Romano.

"Finis."

E

A Century of Bibles.

I.

Oly Bible.
London: Robert Barker.
1611. Folio. Black-letter.

The firſt title is engraved on copper, and ſigned " *Cornelius Boel fecit in Richmont.*" Probably this handſome plate was only iſſued with certain copies: it ſometimes occurs with editions of 1613 and 1617. In the Britiſh Muſeum it is in this edition: while the woodcut title deſcribed below is in the ſecond iſſue of this year. See No. 2. The plate repreſents Moſes and Aaron at either ſide of a Tablet: the four Evangeliſts are below: the Divine name, ſurrounded by rays, above. On the tablet, " The Holy Bible, Conteyning the Old Teſtament and the New: Newly Tranſlated out of the Originall tongues: and with the former Tranſlations diligently compared and reuiſed, by his Maieſties Speciall Cōmandement. Appointed to be read in Churches. Imprinted at London by Robert Barker, Printer to the Kings moſt Excellent Maieſtie. Anno. Dom. 1611." Verſo of title blank. " The Epiſtle Dedicatorie" A 2. ending on A 3 recto. Verſo, " The

Tranflators to the Reader," extending to verfo of B 4.
Kalender fix leaves, C 1, A 2 (*for* C 2), and C 3 with
their followers. An Almanack for 39 years, on D 1.
Table to find Eafter for ever, verfo D 1. Table and Ka-
lendar, D 2. Verfo, proper Leffons. "The names and
order of all the Bookes" on verfo of D 4, printed wholly
in black. Then follow the Genealogies and Map, when
inferted, 18 leaves, with diftinct regifter. The text begins
A 1. The firft chapter of Genefis has an ornamental
initial I cut in wood, reprefenting the Rofe and Thiftle.
The fignatures are continuous to Ccccc 6 verfo, end of
the Apocrypha. The New Teftament title, which reckons
as A 1 of a new Series, is in a woodcut border, reprefenting
the tents and fhields of the 12 Tribes, the 12 Apoftles, and
the 4 Evangelifts with their emblems : "The Newe Teftament of our Lord and Sauiour Jefvs Chrift. ¶ Newly
Tranflated out of the Originall Greeke : and with the
former Tranflations diligently compared and reuifed by
his Maiefties Speciall Commandement. Imprinted at
London by *Robert Barker*, Printer to the Kings moft
Excellent Maieftie Anno Dom. 1611." Ends on verfo,
A a 6. There are altogether 119 fignatures and 714
leaves of text. The preliminary matter has 4 fignatures
and 18 leaves. There are 59 lines in a full column.

Mr. Fry has compared together 70 copies of the Bible
of 1611. By obferving how many of them were exactly
alike he was able to determine their order of publication.
Twenty-three copies were found to prefent the fame pecu-
liarities. Two only varied from the 25 and from each
other, in 8 leaves, 2 in one and 6 in the other. Of the
remaining 45, 40 were mixed with leaves from other
editions, but 38 contained leaves of the fame edition. Mr.
Fry's conclufions were as follows :—One iffue is unmixed
except 2 copies in 25 : the other is made up (1) with reprints (2) with parts of the firft iffue, (3) with preliminary

leaves from 3 other editions : he therefore infers that the two iſſues were diſtinct and that the iſſue which preſented the feweſt inſtances of admixture was the firſt. His concluſions ſeem unaſſailable : it is therefore aſſumed to be proved in this liſt, that the iſſue of which he examined 25 copies ſo nearly alike, is the firſt, and is entitled to the honour of being called the *Editio Princeps* of the verſion.

The following errata will be found, among others, in copies of this Bible :—

Geneſis x. 16. Emorite, *for* Amorite.

Exodusxiv. 10. And when Pharaoh drew nigh
> The children of Iſrael lift up their eyes
> and behold the Egyptians marched af-
> ter them ; and they were ſore afraid : and
> the children of Iſrael lift up their eyes
> and beholde the Egyptians marched
> after them and they were ſore afraid : *repetition.*

Leviticus xii. 56. plaine, *for* plague.

Ruth iii. 15. he went into the citie, *for* ſhe went.

II. Samuel 24. *heading*, eleven thouſand, *for* thirteen hundred thouſand.

II. Chronicles, xxix. *heading*, 39.

Ezra iii. 5. offred, offered, *repetition.*

Micah iv. *heading*, Joel.

I. Eſdras iv. *heading*, Anocrynha, *for* Apocrypha.

St. Matth. xvi. 25. his his, *repetition.*

On the woodcut title to the New Teſtament, as well as on the Old Teſtament woodcut title uſually aſſigned to the ſecond iſſue the line " Appointed to be read in Churches " is omitted.

It may be convenient in this place to enumerate the chief differences of readings which exiſt between this, the *editio princeps* of the preſent Engliſh Bible, and the edition which in 1769 was reviſed by Dr. Blayney and publiſhed at the Oxford Univerſity Preſs, in folio and quarto. The folio edition is very fcarce, it is faid on account of a fire, by which a large number of copies were deftroyed : but more probably becaufe a fmaller number were printed and perhaps fome of thefe fuppreffed on account of the grofs careleffnefs of the printing. In reality, however, this is a matter of little confequence as both folio and quarto were printed from the fame fetting up of type and chiefly differ in the length of the columns. An account of the fteps taken by Dr. Blayney to render this Bible as perfect as poffible may be found in the *Gentleman's Magazine* for 1769, p. 517, and reads ftrangely befide the following lift of errata. Mr. Lea Wilfon's lift is itfelf erroneous and Dr. Cotton had apparently never feen the folio edition as he quotes, from Mr. Horne, the miftaken ftatement that the omiffion in Rev. 18 occurs in the 4to only : although it is to be found in both editions, and was followed in Bibles printed in 1770, Oxf^d folio ; 1772, ditto ; 1772, Oxf^d. 4to. and 1773 ditto. (See Curtis, *Exifting Monopoly*, 1833, p. 90.)

1611.	1769.
II. Kings xxiii. 21. This book of the covenant.	The book of this covenant.
I. Chron. xxix. 6. Over the king's work.	Of the king's work.
Job. iv. 6. Is not this thy feare, thy confidence ; the uprightneffe of thy wayes & thy hope ?	Is not this thy fear, thy confidence, thy hope and the uprightnefs of thy ways ?
Mal. iii. 4. Offerings.	Offering.
S. Matt. xii. 23. Is this the Son.	Is not this the Son.
S. John xxi. 17. He faid.	He faith.
Romans vii. 20. Now if I do.	Now if do.
Romans xii. 2. that acceptable.	and acceptable.

1611.	1769.
I. Cor. iv. 13. World.	Earth.
II. Cor. xii. 2. Above fourteen years.	About fourteen years.
Gal. ii. 6. Thefe who feemed.	Thofe who feemed.
I. Tim. i. 4. Edifying.	Godly edifying.
Heb. xii. 1. run with patience unto the race.	Run with patience the race.
Rev. xviii. 22. And the voyce of harpers and mufitions and of pipers and trumpeters fhall bee heard no more at all in thee: and no crafts man of whatfoever craft hee be fhall be found any more in thee: and the found of a milftone fhal be heard no more at all in thee.	And the voice of harpers and muficians and of pipers and trumpeters fhall be heard no more in thee; and the found of a milftone fhall be heard no more at all in thee.

There are many other paffages in which alterations are made befides the above; the Italics throughout are " re-vifed;" the headings of chapters changed; the fpelling modernized and the punctuation " corrected." It is how-ever queftionable whether all thefe changes were for the better.

2.

Holy Bible.

London : Robert Barker. 1611.

Folio. Black-letter.

The fecond iffue of the year. Leaves of the firft are ufually found mixed in the copies of this iffue. The two read together except in the particulars mentioned below.

The general title is within a woodcut border; at leaſt this
is the title page to be found in ſome copies, and uſually
aſſigned to it; but there is no ground for ſuppoſing that
it was always iſſued with it.   The engraved title ſometimes occurs, but it is moſt frequently found with the woodcut title of 1613: in many copies this date is ingeniouſly
altered into 1611.   So largely has this fraud been practiſed
that Mr. Lenox (*Early Editions*, privately printed, 1861)
doubts the exiſtence of a genuine Old Teſtament title within a woodcut border dated 1611.   Nevertheleſs examples
do exiſt: one is in the Britiſh Muſeum.   Mr. Fry examined
45 copies of this edition: 38 were found to contain leaves
of the firſt iſſue; in 22 inſtances there were R r r, 3 and 4.
In the New Teſtament 15 had S 1 and S 6, and 17 had V,
3, 4.

The chief differences in the collation of this edition
with the previous one are theſe:—The fifth leaf is Sig. B.
in the preliminary matter: Kalender C, C 2, C 3, and
followers.   In the firſt page of the Dedication OE is printed
for OF and in the 8th line CHKIST for CHRIST.   In
the " Names and order of the Bookes " there are three
lines printed in red: 1 Chronicles, is miſprinted 1 Corinthians and 11 Chronicles, 11 Corinthians.   The chief errors
of the firſt iſſue are corrected, but the repetition in Ezra iii.
5, remains.   Exodus ix. 13, Let my people goe that they
may ſerve thee, *for* ſerve me.   S. Matthew xxvi. 36, Then
commeth Judas with them unto a place called Gethſemane,
for Then cometh Jeſus.   The initial P. at Pſalm 112, contains a woodcut of Walſingham's creſt.

3.

THE NEW TESTAMENT of our Lord and
Sauiour Jeſvs Chriſt.   ¶ Newly Tranſlated

out of the Original Greeke : and with the
former Tranflations diligently compared &
reuifed.   By his Maieftie's fpeciall Commandement.   Imprinted at London by
Robert Barker, Printer to the King's moft
Excellent Maieftie.   An. 1611.

¶ Cum priuilegio.   Cor mundum crea
in me Deus, Pfa. 51.   On the reverfe
printed in Roman Letter ¶ The names
and orders of all the Bookes in the New
Teftament, with the Number of their
chapters.

The firft 12*mo*. New Teftament. Black=
letter.

The above account of the title page is taken from Lea
Wilfon, No. 57.   This is the only copy known: it was
bought for Mr. James Lenox of New York for 33*l.* 15*s.*
in 1854.   Mr. Lea Wilfon adds to his account:—" The
text A to A a in 12's except the laft which is 6 only.   It
is beautifully printed in a fharp long black letter; in long
lines, with a black line round the page : the marginal references, which are in Roman type, are divided from the text
by another line.   The initial letters to each book are cut
in wood.   The running titles and chapters are in Roman,
the contents of chapters in Italic letter.   I have never feen
another copy of the book."

4.

THE HOLY BIBLE, conteyning the Old Teftament, and the New : Newly tranflated out
of the Originall tongues & with the former
Tranflations diligently compared and reuifed
by his Maiefties fpeciall Comandement.
Appointed to be read in Churches.

Imprinted at London by Robert Barker,
Printer to the Kings moft Excellent
Maieftie.   Anno Dom.   1612.

The firft *quarto* edition.   Roman Letter.

Title page engraved on copper, within border reduced
from title of folio of 1611.   Signed "Iafpar Ifac, fecit."
The title and introductory matter, 8 leaves with diftinct
regifter : " the names and order of all the Bookes," recto
of *A* 8 : verfo blank.   Genefis begins on A.   Old Teft.
extends to verfo of Ggg 4.   Apocrypha end on Ttt. 6.
Job ends on recto of Kk 4 : verfo blank.   Gen. x. 16.
Emorite for *Amorite*.   Ruth iii. 15.   *Hee*, for *fhe*.   Ezra iii.
5. *offered*, repeated.   New Teft. title within heart-fhaped
woodcut border.   Wants the line " Appointed to be read
in Churches."   The regifter, Ttt. 7. to Zzz 8, (A) to
(M. 8.) ends on recto : verfo blank.   Colophon, 1612.
Heading of (H 5) verfo, " The Galatians reproued.   To
the Galaitans.   The Law a Scholemafter to Chrift."

5.

HOLY BIBLE, conteyning &c.

Imprinted at London by Robert Barker.

1612.

8vo.

> Titles within woodcut heartſhaped borders. No line
> " Appointed to be read in Churches," on either. Dedi-
> cation to King James. No preface. Apocrypha. Firſt
> 8vo. There is at leaſt one varying edition of the ſame
> year: may be diſtinguiſhed by the ornamental headings
> and by A 4 being marked A 2.

6.

Ʈhe New Ʈeſtament of our Lord and
Sauiour Ieſvs Chriſt, ¶ Newly Tranſlated
out of the Originall Greeke: And with
the former Tranſlations diligently compared
and reuiſed, By his Maieſtie's ſpeciall commandement.

¶ Imprinted at London by Robert
Barker, Printer to the Kings moſt Excellent
Maieſtie.   1612.

The firſt *quarto* teſtament.   Black-letter.

> Title within woodcut border: the four Evangeliſts and
> two emblematical figures, *Fides* and *Humilitas*. The royal

arms inferted above, the arms of Elizabeth having been
cut out of the block. Paged, 1—686. The type ufed is
that of the folio of 1613, being fmaller than that of 1611.
St. John xix. 19, tile, *for* title: but generally very correct.
Pages 314 and 342 headed "The Acts," for "The
Actes" as in other places.

<h2 style="text-align:center">7.</h2>

Holy Bible.
London: Robert Barker.   1613-11.
Folio.   Large Black-letter.

This is the fecond folio of 1611, with further alterations and improvements. The titles are both woodcut.
Mr. Lenox afferts, that in all the woodcut firft titles dated
1611, with which he is acquainted, he can detect an alteration of the 1613 into 1611. Mr. Fry, however, defcribes one
or two genuine examples. The Bibles with the above date
are ufually made up of the two editions of 1611, together
with cancels. Sometimes both titles have 1613. But the
fize of the type will immediately diftinguifh this edition
from No. 11.

<h2 style="text-align:center">8.</h2>

HOLY BIBLE.
London: Robert Barker.   1613-12.
4to.   Roman letter.

Title of O. T. in a woodcut heart-fhaped border, dated
1613, wants line *Appointed*, &c.; N. T. title fame, but dated
1612. The fpelling is altered throughout; the errors at

Ruth iii. xv., *Ezra* iii. v. and heading of *Galatians* iii. are corrected, but *Gen.* x. 16, Emorite.   Has the Apocrypha. The two editions generally read together; the chief difference being in the fpelling.   See No. 4.

9.
HOLY BIBLE.
    London: Robert Barker.   1613-12.
8vo.

10.

The Holy Bible, conteyning the Old Teftament and the New: Newly Tranflated out of the Originall tongues: & with former Tranflations diligently compared and reuifed, by his Maiefties fpeciall commandement. ¶ *Appointed to be read in Churches.*
    Imprinted at London by Robert Barker, Printer to the Kings moft excellent Maieftie. Anno Dom.   1613.
Folio.   **Black-letter.**

Both titles are in woodcut borders fimilar to that of 1611.   The line "*Appointed*, &c." is on both.   Firft title followed by Dedication to King James, *fig. A.* 2 : ends on recto of *A* 3. near the top of the page, eleven lines followed by (***).   Tranflators to the Reader, 11 pages, from verfo of *A.* 3. to verfo of *B.* 4.   *Kalender,* 12 pages, regifter *C.* 1. *to C.* 6.   Other preliminary matter, *Sig. D.* 1 *to D* 4.

the names and order of the Books being on the verfo of
the latter. This is correctly printed, the firft line being in
red as well as the words " The Bookes called Apocrypha "
and " The Bookes of the New Teftament." Then, in moft
copies the Genealogies follow. They have a feparate
regifter from *A. 1. to C. 6.* and are paged 1 to 34, the
numbers on pp. 31, and 32, being refpectively 13 and
23. Genefis begins on A. 1. The type is much fmaller
than in the folio of 1611, and the reading differs throughout. Pfalmes begin on K k, Job ending on the 21ft line of
the previous page. The Prophets end on G g g 2, verfo.
Apocrypha end on T t t. 5. recto, verfo being blank.
S. Matthew begins on V v v. 1., the N. T. title being
T. t t. 6. A a a a. 1. is at S. Luke 7. B b b b 3 is mifprinted B b b. 3. Revelation ends on N n n n 4. recto.
Verfo blank. No colophon. The fignatures are in
ternions throughout except the laft which is a double.
There are 72 lines in a page. The typography is exceedingly incorrect. It differs in upwards of 300 places
from the 1ft folio, and although in fome the text is
improved, in the great majority it is altered for the worfe.
The following will ferve as examples :—

Gen. xxvii. 44. paffe, *for* turne.
Levit. vii. 25. faft, *for* fat.
1 Sam. x. 16. water, *for* matter.
1 Kings. iii. 15. and offered peace offerings, *omitted.*
2 Kings. xxii. 3. were, *for* year.
2 Chron. vi. 10. throne, *for* roome.
Nehemiah. x. 31. not leave, *for* leave.
Job. xxix. 3. fhined, *for* walked.
Pfa. xi. 1. flie, *for* flee.
Ezek. xxiii. 7. delighted, *for* defiled.
Hof. vi. 5. hewed, *for* fhewed.
Hab. ii. 5. all nations, and heapeth unto him, *omitted.*
Ecclus. xvi. 13, 14. *The two verfes omitted.*

S. Matt. ii. *heading*, Jefus his mother, *for* Jefus and his mother.

S. Matt. xiii. 8. fome fixty fold, *omitted*.

S. Matt. xvi. 11. I fpake not to you concerning bread, *omitted*.

S. Matt. xxvi. 67. palmes who is of their hands, *two words inferted*.

S. Matt. xxvi. 68. he that fmote, *for* who is he that fmote.

S. John xvi. 13. he *omitted*.

S. John xx. 25. and put my finger into the print of the nails, *omitted*.

Acts xiii. 51. them, and came unto, *omitted*.

1 Cor. xi. 17. I praife you, *for* I praife you not.

1 Cor. xvi. 14. doings, *for* things.

2 Cor. ii. 8. continue, *for* confirm.

2 Tim. 4. 16. may be laid to their charge, *for* may not be laid to their charge.

1 Pet. i. 22. felves, *for* fouls.

Rev. vii. 14. great, *omitted*.

11.

The Holy Bible.

London: Robert Barker. 1613.

4to. The firft in black-letter.

No line " Appointed, &c." on either title-page. Sig. A 4. marked B 4. Woodcut heartfhaped borders to titles. Genefis x. 16. Emorite, *for* Amorite. Ruth iii. 15. He *for* She. Ezra iii. 5. Offered, *repeated*.

12.

HOLY BIBLE.

London: Robert Barker. 1613.

4to. Roman letter.

13.

Holy Bible.
    London : Robert Barker.   1613.
8vo.

14.

Holy Bible.
    London : Robert Barker   1613-14.
4to. Black-letter.

New Teft. title dated 1614. Colophon 1614. Ifaiah
xxviii. 9, " Milke and drawen from the beafts," *for*
" breafts."
This Bible does not differ in appearance from the other
blackletter quartos. There is the ufual heart-fhaped woodcut title to each teftament. Neither has the line " Appointed, &c : " names and order, on recto of A 8. verfo blank.
Text begins recto A, fignatures blackletter A to Sff 8.
Prophets end on recto Ss 6. verfo blank. Apocrypha end
on verfo Eee 2. New Teft. title counts as Eee 3. The
fignature Mmm 4 is in Roman type. The date 1614 in the
colophon is in Arabic numerals.

15.

Holy Bible.
    London : Robert Barker.   1614-13.
4to. Black-letter.

16.

Holy Bible.
    London : Robert Barker.   1614-13.
4to. Roman letter.

17.

HOLY BIBLE.

London : Robert Barker.   1614.

8vo.

Dr. Lee (*Memorial, App. lift*, p. 10) mentions a 12mo. of this date. It is probably the fame as this edition.

18.

The Bible.

London :   Robert Barker.   1614-15.

4to.   Black=letter.

New Teftament dated 1615, colophon 1615.

Remarkable for the omiffion of the word Holy on the title page, which does not otherwife differ from the ufual quarto, being in a woodcut heart-fhaped border.   In defcription, fignatures and other marks it anfwers exactly to the Bible of 1613-14 defcribed above.   Sig. *M m m* 2 in italic type, and fig. M m m 4 in Roman type.   Ifa. xxviii. 9. corrected, but Ifa. lii. numbered iii.

There is a variation which does not differ except in having the title corrected.

19.

Holy Bible.

London :   Robert Barker.   1614-17.

Folio.   Black=letter.

This is the 1617 Bible with a different title.   The title was probably experimental.   It is very fcarce : but Mr. Fry has a copy and one was in Offor's Collection.

F

20.
HOLY BIBLE.

London : Robert Barker.   1615.

4to.

Mentioned by Dr. Lee, (*Memorial : lift, p.* 10) and by
Mr. Curtis (*The exifting Monopoly*, p. 33). Not in Britifh
Mufeum.

21.
HOLY BIBLE.

London : Robert Barker.   1615.

8vo.

No line "Appointed &c." on either title.   Has the
Apocrypha. Colophon, dated 1615, recto Kkk (8).   A
copy in Mr. Fry's collection.

22.
New Teſtament.

London :   Robert Barker.   1615.

4to.   Black-letter.

In Daniell's Catalogue.   Probably the Teftament of
No. 18.

23.
NEW TESTAMENT.

London : Robert Barker.   1615.

12mo. fmall.

This teftament is defcribed on the authority of one in

67

the collection of Mr. Ward, which is dated on the contemporary binding 1615, but wants title and last leaf. S. John xiv. 3, may ye, *for* ye may. Romans viii. 18, Suffering, *for* Sufferings. 1 Tim. iv. 16, for doing this, *for* for in doing this.

24.
HOLY BIBLE.

London: Robert Barker. 1616.

Small folio. Roman Letter.

This is the first folio in Roman or ordinary letter. A large paper copy is in the British Museum. The title-pages, on wood, have a fine design, already used for the Bishop's Bibles, representing Justice and Mercy on either side of the royal arms, Mercy having a sprig of heartsease or pansy in her left hand; the arms of Elizabeth are cut out and those of King James substituted. The lion and unicorn figure below, the latter supplanting Queen Elizabeth's dragon. The initials C. B. (Christopher Barker) remain at the foot. There is no line "*Appointed to be read in Churches*" on either title.

The Dedication is on a 2. The preface begins A 3, and ends on verso b 5. Names and order of the Books, recto b 6, verso b 6. large cut of Adam and Eve in Paradise. Genesis begins recto A. Psalmes, verso N n 2. Sig. N n 3 is marked N n. New Testament ends on verso V u u u 7. Colophon, Robert Barker &c. 1616.

25.
HOLY BIBLE.

London: Robert Barker. 1616.

4to. Roman Letter.

First title on copper, the second woodcut; it and the

N. Teft. title being within the ufual heart-fhaped borders. The words " *Appointed to be read in Churches*" are on the copper-plate title, which is exactly the fame as that of the 4to. of 1612. The print is larger than in that edition and the two do not read together.

    Collation.—Name and order on verfo of woodcut title. Dedication on A 2. Preface on verfo A 3. Genefis begins on A with an ornamental fcroll heading. Pfalmes begin on recto A a 3, with the ufual ornamental heading. Apocrypha ends on verfo of & & 7. The New Teftament ends on verfo of N n n. The colophon is dated 1615.

26.

NEW TESTAMENT.

London : Robert Barker.   1616.

12mo. fmall.

    The fignatures are in five and feven blank. The title is printed. The text is in paragraphs, the verfes being numbered in the margin. Scarce. A copy is in Mr. Ward's collection.

27.

Holy Bible.

London : Robert Barker.   1617.

Folio. Black-letter.

    Titles in woodcut borders; have line "Appointed &c." The dedication is headed with a fmall cut of the Royal arms. In the editions of 1634 and 1640 the fame cut is employed, with the addition of C. R. above. The initial letter of St. Matthew's Gofpel reprefents Neptune; the fame initial letter was ufed in 1611, both iffues, and 1613; in 1634 it is replaced by a conventional ornamental capital.

The initial P at Pfalms xxxv. 112, 113 contains a cut of Walfingham's creft.   The initial I, Pfalms 116, 122, contains a cut of St. John the Evangelift.   Pfalm 148 numbered CLXVIII.   Pfalm 149 numbered CLXIX.   Jeremiah xviii. 3, Whelles, *for* wheels.

28.

HOLY BIBLE.

London : Robert Barker.   1617.

8vo.

Does not differ in general appearance from 8vo. of 1612. Genefis Signature A 3, headed with cut of Eden.   Apocrypha begin recto N n 8, with an ornamental heading. New Teft. title counts as Y y 4.   Ends on recto K k k 8. Colophon dated 1617, verfo blank.   No line " Appointed &c." on either title.

29.

HOLY BIBLE.

London : Robert Barker.   1617.

12mo.

Titles woodcut, with architectural border, and David below.   No line " Appointed " &c. on either.   No chapter headings.   Signatures 5 and feven blank.   Dedication on A.   Names and order of Bookes on verfo.   Genefis begins A 2.   B 3 is marked A 3.   Apocrypha begin Ff 3.   New Teft. title counts as N n (1), ends verfo X x 11.   No colophon.   This is probably the firft edition in 12mo. and is fcarce.   A copy is in the Britifh Mufeum.

30.

HOLY BIBLE.

London : Robert Barker. 1618.

8vo.

Some copies have the New Teft. dated 1617.

31.

HOLY BIBLE.

London : Robert Barker. 1618.

12mo.

Clofely refembles the 12mo. of 1617. Mr. Fry's copy
has a blank leaf marked A. before the title.

32.

HOLY BIBLE.

London : Bonham Norton and John
Bill. 1619.

4to. Roman Letter.

The firft Bible on which Norton and Bill's name appears.
In Lea Wilfon's Catalogue, No. 128 is marked as black-
letter. This is probably an error. The 1ft page of the
dedication has " The Trancelators." The colophon is at
the foot of fig. Gggg 2. recto : and has the names of Norton
and Bill and the date 1619 in Arabic numerals.

33.

HOLY BIBLE.

London : Norton and Bill. 1619.

8vo.

On the back of the title page are the Royal arms in a

garter : without supporters or initials. Mr. Fry's copy has
1618 in the colophon. He has an Old Testament only with
1619 on the title and a different shield of arms on the back.
The signatures are the same in both, and they read together,
but the setting up differs in several places.

34.
HOLY BIBLE.
London : Norton and Bill. 1619.
12mo.

35.
NEW TESTAMENT.
London : Norton and Bill. 1619.
12mo. very small.

Title, woodcut, arch with pillars, figures of the four
evangelists being in the corners. No colophon. Reg. A 2-
Y 12. verso. Called a 16mo. by Lowndes: p. 2633.

36.
Holy Bible.
London : Norton and Bill. 1619-20.
4to. Black-letter.

The New Testament title has the names of *Robert Barker*
and *John Bill* and the date 1620. The colophon has the
name of *Robert Barker* only, and the date 1620 in Arabic
numerals. Verso of G g g 6. heading " S. Matthew" *for*
" S. Marke." The New Testament ends on recto of S ff 8.

This edition and those of the succeeding years to 1625
are often found mixed together in the same volume. It is

almoft if not quite impoffible wholly to diftinguifh them. This edition fometimes occurs with the Dedication " The Trancelators &c." which is here affigned to the iffue of 1619-20-24. Moft of Barker's black-letter quartos read together.

A variation (Mr. Fry) has Colophon 1614.

37.

Holy Bible.
    London : Norton and Bill. 1619-20-24.
4to. **Black-letter.**

The Old Teftament title has *Norton and Bill.* 1619. The dedication is headed *The Trancelators.* The New Teftament title has the names of *Barker and Bill* and the date 1620. The Colophon which is on R r r 8, in the centre of the recto, has *Norton and Bill* and the date 1624 in Roman numerals. On the verfo of fignature P p p 2, II Coainthians is printed for II Corinthians in the heading. This fignature too, is a misprint for O o o which follows it, and P p p is repeated and is followed by *P p p* 3. in italics. 1 Cor. xiii. 5. " Thinketh not." Romans xiii. heading " Romans:" *ufually* " Romanes."

38.

Holy Bible.
    London : Norton and Bill. 1620.
8vo.

There is a copy in Mr. Fry's collection.

39.

HOLY BIBLE.

London: Barker and Bill. 1620.

12mo.

Titles within ufual architectural border. No line "Appointed &c." on either. Genefis begins A 2. Prophets end verfo F f 2. New Teft. title counts as N n 1. Revelation ends on verfo X x (11). The colophon is on recto X x 12. between two woodcut ornaments. Verfo blank.

40.

Holy Bible.

London: Norton and Bill. 1620-21

4to. Black-letter.

The preface is headed EHE, *for* THE. Sig. D 4. is marked erroneoufly C 4. The verfe of P p p. 2 is headed II Coainthians, *for* II Corinthians. The New Teftament title is dated 1621. The Colophon is on S f f 8. and has the date 1621 in Roman numerals. S. Mark xiv. 46, on *omitted*. There is alfo a variation with the heading of the preface corrected.

41.

HOLY BIBLE.

London: Norton and Bill. 1621.

8vo.

No line "Appointed &c." on either title-page. No printer's name on New Teftament Title.

42.
New Testament.
    London : Norton and Bill.   1621.
12mo.   **Black-letter.**

43.
Holy Bible.
    London : Norton and Bill.   1622.
8vo.

44.
Holy Bible.
    London : Norton and Bill.   1622-23.
4to.

> Colophon, 1623. 60 lines to a column. Gen. 1. on
> Sig. A. Apocrypha end on recto C c c (5). The New
> Testament title counts as P p p 1. Colophon on G g g g 2,
> recto. Verso blank. Mr. Fry has a copy. There is a
> variation edition in which the New Test. title is dated
> 1623.

45.
New Testament.
    London : Norton and Bill.   1622.
12mo.   **Black-letter.**

> L. W. (No. 69) mentions a similar Testament of 1623.

46.

HOLY BIBLE.

London: Norton and Bill.   1623.

8vo.

Scarce. Not in the collections of the B. M. the Bodleian, of Mr. Ewing or Mr. Fry. L. W. No. 133. Isa. liii. 10. plased *for* pleased. S. Luke ii. 2. tazed *for* taxed. Lee mentions a 12mo.; probably this.

47.

HOLY BIBLE.

London: Norton and Bill.   1624.

8vo.

Very similar to the preceding Bibles of this size—1612, &c.

48.

HOLY BIBLE.

London: Norton and Bill.   1624.

12mo.

49.

Holy Bible.

London: Norton and Bill.   1625.

4to. Black-letter.

There is a variation in which the colophon is dated 1624. See note to No. 36.

50.

HOLY BIBLE.

London : Norton and Bill.   1625.

8vo.

There are two variations of this edition, without printers'
name or place. Perhaps foreign.

51.

HOLY BIBLE.

London : Norton and Bill.   1625.

12mo.

52.

NEW TESTAMENT.

London : Norton and Bill.   1625.

8vo. very fmall : apparently 24mo.

Woodcut title. Arms of Queen Elizabeth : lion and
dragon, below : Juftice and Mercy above. Order of the
Books, verfo of title. Regifter A 2—G g 5. No colophon.
On verfo of laft page begins " The Epiftles of the Old Teftament according as they bee now read." Thefe are Joel
2. Efay 63. Efay 5. Jere. 23. Efay 7. Efay 40 ; being the
portions appointed *for the Epiftle* on certain days.

This is probably the New Teftament called 32mo. in
Lea Wilfon. It has the following mifprints, among
others :—St. Mark 11, *heading* Mare. Eph. ii. 4. God is
rich in mercy, *for* God who is rich in mercy. 11 Pet. i. 8.
in you and bound, *for* in you and abound. 11 John 7. is,
repeated.

53.
New Testament.
   London : Norton and Bill.   1625.
  12mo. **Black-letter.**

54.
Holy Bible.
   London : Norton and Bill.   1626.
  8vo.
     There is a variation of this edition.

55.
Holy Bible.
   London : Norton and Bill.   1626.
  12mo.

56.
New Testament.
   London : Norton and Bill.   1626.
  18mo. **Black-letter.**
     Lea Wilson, No. 71.

57.
New Testament.
   London : Norton and Bill.   1626.
  12mo. small.

58.
HOLY BIBLE.
London : Norton and Bill.   1627.
4to.

Text begins A. (1) C c c 4 verſo end of Prophets. O o o
(8) verſo, end of Apocrypha.   New Teſt. title counts at
P p p (1).   Revelation ends reƈto G g g g 2, which is
unſigned.   Colophon 1627 in Roman numerals.

59.
HOLY BIBLE.
London : Norton and Bill.   1627.
8vo.

60.
NEW TESTAMENT.
London : Norton and Bill.   1627.
12mo.

61.
New Teſtament.
London : Norton and Bill.   1627.
Small 8vo : ſize of 12mo.   Black-letter.
Long lines.   L. W. 72.

62.
Holy Bible.
London : Norton and Bill.   1628.
4to.   Black-letter.

63.

Holy Bible.

London: Norton and Bill. 1628.

8vo.

Titles within heart-fhaped woodcut. Cut of Adam and Eve in Eden, heading Genefis i. Apocrypha begin N n 8 recto, with cut of *David* for heading. The catch-word of the previous page is PO for APO. Apoc. end Y y 3 verfo. New Teft. title counts as Y y 4. Revelation ends recto K k k 8. Colophon 1628. There are two other flightly varying iffues of this year in 8vo.

64.

New Testament.

London : Norton and Bill. 1628.

24mo.

This edition was in Offor's Collection. It is not in the Britifh Mufeum.

65.

New Teftament.

London: Norton and Bill. 1628.

8vo. Black=letter.

Engraved title. Architectural ornaments, with pillars; two emblematical figures, and the four Evangelifts. The Order of the Books, printed on verfo. Reg. A 2—E e 8, verfo. Long lines.

This is probably the edition called by Lowndes a 24mo. See Bibliographer's Manual, part 9, p. 2633.

66.

NEW TESTAMENT.

Edinburgh : Heirs of Hart.   1628.

Small 8vo.

"Newlie Tranflated &c. by His Majefties fpeciall comandement. Edinb. by the heires of Andro Hart." See Lowndes, p. 2633. A Calendar was inferted. The Table of Moveable Feafts includes only *Whitfunday*, *Eafter-day*, and the beginning of *Lentron*. It is the firft Scottifh New Teftament of this verfion and very fcarce.

67.

NEW TESTAMENT.

Cambridge : By the Printers to the Uni-verfitie.   1628.

12mo.   Small.

Plain printed title. Cambridge device on verfo Y 12. Lowndes, p. 2633. There is a fmall Teftament in the Britifh Mufeum, without a date on the title ; it is the fame as this one except in title. It is defcribed under 1630.

68.

HOLY BIBLE.

London : Norton and Bill.   1629.

Folio.   Roman letter.

Engraved firft title by Ifac. Scarce.

69.

HOLY BIBLE.
London: Norton and Bill. 1629.
4to.

70.

HOLY BIBLE.
London: Norton and Bill. 1629.
8vo.

71.

HOLY BIBLE.
London: Norton and Bill. 1629.
12mo.

The Apocrypha are included in the "Names and order of books," but feldom occur in copies.

72.

HOLY BIBLE.
Cambridge: Thomas and John Buck.
Small folio. Roman letter. 1629.

Lea Wilfon fays, of this edition, "The text appears to have undergone a complete revifion, although I can find no record of fuch having been done by authority. Yet the errors in the firft and intermediate editions are here corrected, and confiderable care appears to have been exercifed as to

G

the words printed in italics, punctuation," &c. The title
is engraved on copper; it was afterwards used for quarto
Bibles and has here a wide margin. This feems to be the
firft Bible in which the mifprint occurs: 1 Tim. iv. 16,
Take heed unto thyfelf and unto *thy* doctrine, for *the* doctrine. There are many other alterations, fome of them not
improvements. (See *Cardwell.*) In the Lambeth Library
is a copy of the New Teftament of this edition, printed on
one fide only: another copy is in the Britifh Mufeum.

73.

Holy Bible.

London: Norton and Bill.   1630.

4to. **Black-letter.**

74.

Holy Bible.

London: Barker and Bill.   1630.

4to. **Black-letter.**

75.

Holy Bible.

London: Robert Barker and the affigns
of John Bill.   1630.

4to. Roman letter large.

Dated throughout 1630. Lea Wilfon's copy in Britifh
Mufeum.

76.

HOLY BIBLE.
London: Barker and affignes of Bill.
8vo.   1630.
L. W. No. 143, appendix.

77.

HOLY BIBLE.
London: Norton and Bill.   1630.
8vo.

78.

NEW TESTAMENT.
London: Barker and Affigns of Bill.
12mo.   1630.

79.

NEW TESTAMENT.
London: Barker and Affigns of Bill.
12mo. fmall.   1630.
The fignatures run in five and feven blanks.

80.

Holy Bible.

> Cambridge : T. and J. Buck. 1630.
> 4to.

> 1 Tim. iv. 16, Thy.

81.

Holy Bible.

> Cambridge : T. and J. Buck. 1630.
> 4to. Black-letter.

The firſt title is engraved. It is the ſame as that of the folio of 1629. 1 Tim. iv. 16 : Thy doɕtrine, *for* the doctrine.

82.

New Testament.

> Cambridge : (T. and J. Buck.) n. d.
> 12mo. ſmall.

In Brit. Mus. Catalogue this teſtament is marked 24mo. as it was in the Suſſex Catalogue, from which Colleɕtion it came. It has alſo *London ?* 1630 ? in the B. M. Catalogue. As it has the Cambridge printer's device on the laſt leaf, there can be no doubt of its origin. The title is engraved with the Nativity. On a curtain above, " The Newe Teſtament," &c. Space below, for date and name, left blank. Verſo of title, " Order of Books." Text, A 2—Y 12. On verſo of laſt leaf, Cambridge device. Except in the title this N. T. agrees exaɕtly with the N. T. of 1628 in Mr. Ward's colleɕtion. See No. 67.

83.

HOLY BIBLE.

London : Barker and Aſſignes of Bill.

8vo.   1631-30.

Engraved title-page. No Apocrypha. New Teſtament
title has an architectural deſign, with *Fides* and *Religio* on
each ſide, and at the foot David playing the harp. Colophon dated 1630. There are ſeveral varieties of this edition.
Mr. Fry has three. See No. 86.

84.

HOLY BIBLE.

London : Barker and Aſſignes of Bill.

8vo.   1631.

This is uſually called by the name of the " Wicked
Bible," on account of the miſprint in Exodus xx. 14,
" Thou ſhalt commit adultery," *for* " Thou ſhalt not." In
the Britiſh Muſeum copy the following note is in pencil on
the fly leaf :—

" Only one other copy is known. I ſold it to Mr. Lenox
of New York in July laſt for £52 10s. 0d.; that copy is
perfect, and this one agrees with it leaf for leaf, *except the
twenty-three leaves wanting in this.* A thouſand copies of
this bible were printed, but being found to be full of groſs
typographical errors, the King's printers, Meſſrs. Barker
and Lucas, were ſummoned before the high commiſſion
court and fined £300, and the entire edition was ordered to
be deſtroyed. There were two, if not three, other editions
in octavo in 1631 by the ſame printers cloſely reſembling

this, but reprinted throughout. The error in the 7th commandment is only one of a thoufand.—HENRY STEVENS.

"Leaves fupplied, October, 1861."

Lowndes (*Bibliographer's Manual*, vol. i. p. 186, Bohn's
edition) erroneoufly ftates that this Bible was printed in
1632. A very full notice of it and of the other octavos of
1631, may be found in *Notes and Queries*, 2nd S. vol. v. p.
389, in a letter from Neo Eboracenfis (? Mr. Lenox).
He fays, "I cannot account for the infertion of the name
of 'Lucas' in many of the notices of the fuppreffed volume.
That name is not found, I believe, in the imprint of any
Bibles of the period fpecified."

Copies of this Bible are in the Britifh Mufeum (c. 24. a),
in the Bodleian at Oxford, in the collection of Mr. Lenox
as mentioned above, and in that of William Euing, Efq.,
Glafgow.

A copy (Mr. Lenox's) was exhibited to the Society of
Antiquaries, June 25, 1855, by Mr. Stevens. The title to
the Old Teftament is printed within a heart-fhaped woodcut, date 1631. The fignatures run in eights. The Apocrypha is included. The New Teftament title fimilar, and
dated 1631. Colophon, dated 1631. Mr. Euing's copy
wants the Apocrypha, which that in the Britifh Mufeum
has.

85.

HOLY BIBLE.

London : Robert Barker and Affignes of
John Bill.   1631.

8vo.

Another edition in which the chief errors are corrected.
Like the foregoing, it does not materially differ in fize or

appearance from the ordinary octavos of this period, of which the firft was printed in 1612. The New Teftament title and the colophon are dated 1631.

86.

HOLY BIBLE.

London : Robert Barker and Affignes of Bill. 1631-30-31.

8vo.

The fame, but with the New Teftament title dated 1630. The colophon has 1631.

There are many other varieties of this 8vo. Some have 1630 in the colophon, fome 1632. Others have the New Teft. dated 1632. All read together. Mr. Fry has feven varieties with 1631 on the Old Teft. title.

87.

HOLY BIBLE.

London : Robert Barker and Affignes of John Bill. 1631.

12mo.

The date in the colophon is in Roman numerals.

88.

New Teftament.

London : Robert Barker and Affignes of John Bill. 1631.

4to. Black-letter.

Clofely refembles 4to. of 1612 : it has the fame number of pages :—686.

89.
𝔑ew 𝔗eſtament.
London: Barker and Aſſignes of Bill.
12mo. long lines.   𝔅lack-letter·   1631.

90.
HOLY BIBLE.
London: Barker and Aſſignes of Bill.
4to.   1632-30.

91.
𝔥oly 𝔅ible.
London: Barker and Aſſignes of Bill.
4to.   𝔅lack-letter.   1632-31.

Colophon dated 1631. The regiſter is continuous,
Geneſis i. being on 𝔄 1. and the Pſalmes commencing
on 𝔈 c 2. in the centre of the recto. Apocrypha begin on
𝔖 ß 7. recto, the verſo of 𝔖 6 being blank. The New
Teſtament title counts as 𝔈 c c 3. and S. Matt. i. is on
𝔈 c c 4. Rom. xiv. 1. Receive you, *for* ye.
There are two ſlightly differing iſſues. Compare the
headings of Deut. i. and of 1 Kings i.

92.
HOLY BIBLE.
London: Barker and Aſſigns of Bill.
12mo.   1632-31-31.

A variation has 1633 N. T. title.

93.

HOLY BIBLE.

London : Barker &c.   1632.

Small folio.   Roman letter.

94.

𝕳𝖔𝖑𝖞 𝕭𝖎𝖇𝖑𝖊.

London : Barker &c.   1632.

4to.   𝕭𝖑𝖆𝖈𝖐-𝖑𝖊𝖙𝖙𝖊𝖗.

95.

HOLY BIBLE.

London : Barker &c.   1632.

8vo.

There are at leaſt four varieties of this 8vo.

96.

NEW TESTAMENT.

London : Barker &c.   1632.

Folio.

This is probably not a ſeparate book, but part of the folio Bible of ſame year. It is mentioned in Lowndes, p. 2633.

97.

HOLY BIBLE.

London: Barker &c.   1633-32.

Folio.   Roman letter.

Firſt title engraved by Hole (for deſcription ſee under
1639). Dedication A 2. Tranſlator's preface A 3, verſo
A (8.). Names and order of books A (9.) reƈto. view of
Eden, verſo. Text A (1) to H h h (5.) verſo, end oſ
Prophets. The Apocrypha begin reƈto H h h (6.) with a
heading: ends X x x 4. reƈto. Verſo blank. New Teſt.
title dated 1632. Woodcut border, "Juſtice and Mercy,"
&c. Colophon on verſo P p p p (5.) 1632. This deſcription is made from the copy at Syon College. Sig. R 2
for X 2.

98.

HOLY BIBLE.

London: Barker &c.   1633.

4to.

99.

HOLY BIBLE.

London: Barker &c.   1633.

8vo.

100.

HOLY BIBLE.

London: Barker &c.   1633.

12mo.

Mr. Fry's copy has the rare firſt page Sig. A. before the
title. Colophon on ſeparate leaf.

101.

NEW TESTAMENT.

London : Barker and Affigns of Bill.

4to. 1633.

102.

NEW TESTAMENT.

London : Barker &c. 1633.

24mo. or 32mo.

103.

𝕳oly 𝕭ible.

Cambridge : Buck and Daniel. 1633.

4to. 𝕭lack-letter.

There are at leaft two varieties of this edition. They differ but flightly.

104.

HOLY BIBLE.

Edinburgh : printed by the printers to the King's moft excellent Majeftie : cum privilegio. 1633.

8vo.

The firft Bible printed in Scotland. Moft copies have many engravings. It was a charge againft Archbifhop Laud that he brought Popifh pictures from beyond the fea. See *Lord Hailes's Letters*, where they are defcribed

as " abominable " and as " horrible impiety." Some of
them neverthelefs are very good, and not unworthy of the
advanced ftate of Art at the time in Holland, whence they
probably came. They are faid to have been firft printed
by Boetius a Bolfwert in 1623. See Dr. Lee's *Memorial*,
p. 97.

The titlepage is engraved : Mofes and Aaron fupport
between them a book on which is written " THE HOLY
BIBLE, *containing the Old Teftament and the New : Newly
tranflated out of the originall and with the former diligently
compared and revifed by his Majefties fpeciall commandement.
Appointed to be read in Churches. Edinburgh, printed by the
printers to the Kings moft excellent Majeftie.*" On a fcroll
below, " *Cum Privilegio. Anno Dom.* 1633." Below this
is a figure of Jeffe from whom a branch proceeds bearing,
as a border to the page, the emblems of the tribes and prophets. The Triangular fymbol of the Trinity is above in
clouds, with the Holy Name in Hebrew. At the four
corners of the plate are the figures of the Evangelifts in
ovals. Moft copies have a frontifpiece reprefenting Adam
and Eve in Paradife. The title is followed by a blank page :
on the verfo of the leaf is the royal fhield within a garter.
This leaf is often miffing. The dedication is on A 2. in
the third line " *Brittain*" is the fpelling. The name and
order of the books is on the verfo. Text begins on A 3.
Pfalmes begin on verfo of Z 2. Firft five pfalms on the page.
Malachi ends N n, 8. Apocrypha O o 1, to Y y 4. The
New Teftament title has a conventional border : the date
1633. On the back of the titlepage are the arms of Scotland, quartering France with England, in the fecond place,
and Ireland, in the third, within a garter. S. Matt. begins
A a a 1. New Teft. ends on recto M m m 4. The arms
laft defcribed are repeated on the verfo. 1 Tim. iv. 16, reads
" Thy " *for* " the."

The number of efcutcheons and the generally handfome

appearance of the volume give colour to the affertion which has been fometimes made that it was printed for the Coronation of Charles I., in Scotland, which took place in 1633.

There is a variation iffue, differing flightly. Mr. Fry has both.

105.
NEW TESTAMENT.

Edinburgh : King's Printers.   1633. 8vo.

This is the New Teftament of the Bible of the fame date. It fhould not be called a feparate publication as there is no table of the books : but it appears to have been iffued feparately.

106.
NEW TESTAMENT.

Edinburgh : Robert Young.   1633. 8vo.

Young was the King's Printer, and there is little but the title to diftinguifh this edition from the laft. The Royal arms are omitted.

107.
NEW TESTAMENT.

London : Auguftine Matthews.   1633. Folio.

This is Fulke's edition, the verfion of 1611 being fubftituted for that of 1568. The Rhemes tranflation is in parallel columns with it.

108.

HOLY BIBLE.

London : Robert Barker and affigns of J.
Bill.   1633-33-34.
    4to.
            Colophon 1634.

109.

Holy Bible.

London : Barker and Affigns of Bill.
                                              1634.
Folio. Black=letter.

Among the marks by which this edition may be diftinguifhed from its predeceffors is the reading in Heb. xii. 1,
runne with patience the race, *for* runne with patience unto
the race, as in 1611 and 1617. The initial B in Pfalm 1,
contains a cut of Cecil's arms. The initial P at Pfalm 35,
has Walfingham's creft as in 1617.

110.

Holy Bible.

London : Barker and Affigns of Bill.
4to. Black=letter.   1634.

1 Tim. iv. 16, Thy, *for* the. There are three varieties.
Mr. Fry has them, and alfo one with 1636 New Teftament
Title.

111.
HOLY BIBLE.

London : Barker and Affigns of Bill.

8vo. 1634.

There are two or three varieties (Mr. Fry). One of them has 1635 O. T. title.

112.
HOLY BIBLE.

London : Barker and Affigns of Bill.

12mo. 1634.

113.
HOLY BIBLE.

Edinburgh. 1634.

12mo.

114.
HOLY BIBLE.

London : Barker and Affigns of Bill.

8vo. 1635.

115.

HOLY BIBLE.

London : Barker and Affigns of Bill.

12mo.   1635.

Titles within Architectural border : with King David and the text " Cor mundum," &c. Apocrypha. New Teft. title counts as P p (1). No chapter headings. The B. M. copy wants the Apocrypha. Colophon on Z z (12) verfo.

116.

New Teſtament.

London : Barker and Affigns of Bill.

8vo.   Blackletter.   1635.

117.

NEW TESTAMENT.

London : Barker and Affignes of Bill.

12mo.   1635.

A 16mo. is named in fome catalogues. 1 Tim. iv. 16, Thy.

118.

Holy Bible.

Cambridge : Thomas Buck and Roger Daniel.   1635.

4to.   Black-letter.

119.

HOLY BIBLE.

Cambridge: T. Buck and R. Daniel.

4to.   1635.

120.

𝔑ew 𝔗eſtament.

Edinburgh: Robt. Young.   1635.

12mo.   𝔅lack=letter.

121.

HOLY BIBLE.

London: Barker and Affignes of Bill.

8vo.   1636-34.

There are two ſlightly differing iſſues of this edition.

122.

HOLY BIBLE.

London: Barker and Afligns of Bill.

4to.   1636.

123.

HOLY BIBLE.

London: Barker and Affigns of Bill.

8vo.   1636.

There are at leaſt five varieties (Mr. Fry).

H

124.

NEW TESTAMENT.
Edinburgh : Robert Young. 1636.
8vo.

Properly belongs to the Bible of the following year :
but like the New Teftament of 1633 appears to have been
iffued feparately. The back of the title is blank. Signatures run from A a a 2—M m m 4. recto, and a woodcut
of the arms of Scotland, quartering England, France and
Ireland, with a garter is on the verfo. There is no line
" Appointed &c." on the title. Copies are ufually illuftrated with engravings : fee No. 104.

125.

NEW TESTAMENT.
Edinburgh : R. Young. 1636.
32mo.

L. W. No. 79. Lowndes fays it formed part of the
Bible of the following year—but as the Bible was in
8vo. this is not likely. This N. T. is more correctly
called a 12mo.

126.

HOLY BIBLE.
London : Barker and Affignes of Bill.
4to. 1637.

127.

HOLY BIBLE.

London : Barker and Affignes of Bill.

8vo. 1637.

There are at leaft four varieties of this edition : copies of them all are in Mr. Fry's collection. They vary moft often in the title-pages and in the pofition of the fignatures. All read together.

128.

HOLY BIBLE.

London : Barker and Affigns of Bill.

12mo. 1637.

There are at leaft two iffues of this edition. One of them (No. 160 in Lea Wilfon) has "Affigns" on the title-page, inftead of the ufual "Affignes."

129.

New Testament.

London : R. Barker and Affignes of John Bill. 1637.

16mo. Black-letter.

1 Tim. iv. 16. Thy, *for* the. Scarce. A copy was in Mr. Dix's collection. No. 399 in his catalogue.

130.

HOLY BIBLE.

Cambridge: T. Buck and R. Daniel.

4to.   1637.

The Apocrypha has diſtinct ſignatures. Careleſsly printed. St. Matthew xii. 42. "The queen of the South ſhall up," *for* "ſhall riſe up." 1 Tim. iv. 16. "Thy," *for* "the."   St. Matt. i. 25 " he called his ſonne," *for* " he called his name."   The pages are numbered, a freſh ſeries commencing for each part.   In the Bodleian Catalogue it is aſſerted that Field re-iſſued this edition in 1648. See No. 203.

131.

Holy Bible.

Cambridge : Printed by the Printers to the Univerſitie.   1637.

4to.   Black-letter.

The ſignatures are in black-letter. Text begins 𝔄. 1. the preliminary leaves being ſigned with ¶. No colophon. The titles have only black lines and are very plain. 1 Tim. iv. 16. " Thy."

132.

HOLY BIBLE.

Cambridge : Buck and Daniel.   1637.

8vo.

Two iſſues : regiſter various.

133.

HOLY BIBLE.

Edinburgh. 1637.

8vo.

In the Britiſh Muſeum copy the New Teſt. title is dated 1633. Does not differ materially from the edition of 1633; but has no leaf with Royal Arms after firſt title. Apocrypha. Plate of Eden as Frontiſpiece. 1 Tim. iv. 16. Thy, *for* the doctrine.

134.

HOLY BIBLE.

London: Barker, &c. 1637-36.

8vo.

135.

HOLY BIBLE.

London: Barker, &c. 1637-38.

4to.

Apocrypha in ſmaller type. 1 Tim. iv. 16, " Thy." New Teſtament title and colophon 1638. There is a variation edition which differs ſlightly.

136.

HOLY BIBLE.

London: Barker, &c. 1637-37-38.

12mo.

Colophon 1638.

137.
Holy Bible.
> Cambridge : Buck and Daniel. 1637-38.
4to.
> There is no date on the firſt title. The New Teſt. title
> 1637, colophon 1638. Mr. Fry has two copies which differ
> from each other in the firſt leaf of the Tranſlatours preface.
> The errors in the New Teſt. of 1637 are correēted except
> 1 Tim. iv. 16 Thy, *for* the.

138.
Holy Bible.
> London : Barker and Aſſignes of Bill.
> Folio.   1638.
See No. 148.

139.
Holy Bible.
> London: Barker and Aſſignes of Bill.
> 8vo.   1638.
> There are at leaſt three varieties of this year and ſize.

140.
Holy Bible.
> London : Barker and Aſſigues of Bill.
> 12mo.   1638.
> Full of errors. Lea Wilſon enumerates the principal as
> follows :—

Gen. i. 26. Let us make men, *for*, man.

Gen. xxxvii. 2. fons of Belial, *for* Bilhah.

Num. xxv. 18. vex you with their wives, *for* wiles.

Num. xxvi. 10. two thoufand and fifty, *for* hundred and fifty.

II *Sam.* xxiii. 20. flew two lions like men, *for* lion like men.

I *Chron.* xxxiv. 2. that which was evill, *for* that which was right.

I *Chron.* xxxvi. 14. had polluted, *for*, had hallowed.

Nehem. iv. 9. read our prayer, *for* made our prayer.

Ifa. i. 6. purifying fores, *for* putrifying fores.

Ifa. xxix. 13. taught by the people, *for* taught by the precepts.

Ifa. xlix. 22. their fons, *for* thy fons.

Ezek. v. 11. any piety, *for* any pity.

S. Luke vii. 47. her fins which are many are forgotten, *for* forgiven.

S. Luke xix. 29. ten of his difciples, *for* two.

S. John xviii. 29. Pilate went not, *for* went out.

I *Cor.* vii. 34. praife her hufband, *for* pleafe.

I *Tim.* ii. 9. fhamefulneffe, *for* fhamefaftnefs.

I *Tim.* iv. 16. Thy, *for* the.

There is a variation in which " Affignes " is the fpelling on O. T. title. Both probably printed in Holland.

141.

HOLY BIBLE.

London : Barker &c. 1638.

12mo.

May be diftinguifhed by having black lines round each page. There are three variations.

142.

New Testament.
London : Barker &c.   1638.
12mo. Black-letter.

143.

NEW TESTAMENT.
London : Barker &c.   1638.
12mo. fmall.
1 Tim. iv. 16. Thy *for* the.

144.

NEW TESTAMENT.
London : Barker.   1638.
24mo.
Offor, 48mo. Probably the fame as foregoing.

145.

HOLY BIBLE.
Cambridge :   T. Buck and R. Daniel.
Folio.   1638.

Engraved title—*William Marfhall, fculp.*—reprefenting
Mofes and Aaron on either fide ; a picture of Creation above ;
the laft fupper and an illuftration of Pfalm xlii. 1. below ;
the four Evangelifts at the foot. Not dated.

The text is in Roman letter, rather fmall, but clear.
Dedication A 1. and verfo. Tranflatours preface A 2. to
A 5. recto. Names and order of Books, A. 5. verfo.
Genefis begins A 6. Second leaf is B. There is a heading

to the Apocrypha, which begins on fig. K K K, recto.
The New Teſtament title is plainly printed within a conventional border, and is dated 1638.   The text begins freſh
ſignatures, St. Matthew being on A 2.   Revelation ends on
verſo of R 6.   There is no colophon.

In this edition ſeveral new readings occur.   St. Matt.
xii. 23.   Is not this the Son of David : the *not* was omitted
in 1611. 1 John v. 12, hath not the Son of God hath not,
&c., *for* hath not the Son, hath not, &c. 1 Tim. iv. 16.
Thy doctrine, *for* the doctrine.   Acts vi. 3. Whom ye
may appoint, *for* whom we may appoint.   The laſt two
readings are not improvements.   The firſt of them had been
introduced in the Cambridge Bible of 1629.   The ſecond
appears firſt in this edition and was frequently repeated.
It is often erroneouſly aſcribed to the Puritans.   It cer-
tainly occurs after this date in many Bibles ſuppoſed to be
printed for them.   Numbers lxiv., Ram, *for* Lamb.

This edition is ſaid by moſt authorities to have been
reviſed by the ſpecial command of Charles I.   It differs from
the firſt folios chiefly in the uſe made of italics : the following examples are taken from Biſhop Turton (*Text of the
Engliſh Bible*, 2nd Ed. 1833):—

St. Matt. xxvi. 2. After two days is *the feaſt of* the Paſſ-
over, *for* the feaſt of, &c.

Hebrews vii. 24. This *man* becauſe he continueth, *for*
this man.

Hebrews ix. 6. The ſervice *of God, for* of God.

St. Luke xix. 1. *Jeſus* entered *for* Jeſus entered.

Geneſis xviii. 28. all the city for *lack of* five, *for* lack of five.

Judges v. 30, *meet* for the necks, *for* meet for the necks.

Deuteronomy xvi. 10, give *unto the* LORD *thy God for*
unto the LORD thy God.

Many other examples may be found in the ſame book.
This edition is mentioned there with commendation, and
moſt of the alterations are allowed to be improvements.

The credit of the revifion is affigned to Ward, Goad, Boyfe, Mead, and others: and is faid to have taken place *Mandato Regio:* while the refult formed the ftandard Bible until 1769.

146.

HOLY BIBLE.

Edinburgh: Robert Young.   1638.

32mo.

Lowndes, vol. i. p. 187.

147.

NEW TESTAMENT.

Edinburgh: Robert Young.   1638.

32mo.

A copy was in Offor's collection.   It appears to be part of the foregoing Bible.

148.

HOLY BIBLE.

London: Barker and Affignes of Bill.

1639-38-39.

Folio.

The following defcription is of the Britifh Mufeum copy: it is apparently not quite genuine. Title engraved by Holl. An arch flanked by columns, each column wreathed with a vine tree, on one fide fmall vignettes at each inter-lacement of the branches, with the tents of the 12 tribes: at the other the 12 apoftles. At the top of the column firft named, the figure of Mofes receiving the Tables of the

Law : on the other, the Transfiguration : between the
columns and the arch are the emblems of the Evangelists :
the keyftone has a reprefentation of the facrifice of Ifaac.
Above this is a globe, with the Laft Judgment reprefented
upon it : above it, again, the facred name in Hebrew. The
columns reft on bafes containing fmall views of the Temp-
tation in Eden and the Refurrection ; between them, in
front of the arch, is the Man of Sorrows, treading the Wine-
prefs, " Ego torcular calcavi folus." The title is within
the arch and runs in the ufual form. This plate had been
ufed for the Genevan Bible of 1607.

The names and order of the books follow in Roman
type on recto of an unfigned leaf : a woodcut view of Paradife on verfo. Dedication on following page * (1). Tranflators' preface on * 2. four leaves, on verfo of laft Names and
order of books again, but in italics. Genefis begins on A (1.)
Apocrypha on N n n (1.) near the foot of the recto, the
Prophets ending juft above. New Teftament title in woodcut border, " Juftice and Mercy." No line " Appointed,"
&c. Dated 1638. 1 Tim. iv. 16, Thy, for the. Colophon
verfo Y y y y 4. Date in Roman numerals 1639.

149.
Holy Bible.
London : Barker &c. 1639.
Folio.
New Teft. title 1639.

150.
Holy Bible.
London : Barker &c. 1639.
4to.
1 Tim. iv. 16. Thy for the.

151.

HOLY BIBLE.

London : Barker and Affignes of Bill.

8vo. 1639.

On the reverfe of the title of this rare Bible are the royal arms, fupported by a lion and unicorn, without initials. The dedication is on A 2. The names and order on the verfo. A woodcut of Eden at the head of A 3, followed by Gen. i. The heading of II Chronicles xxi. is *Chronicles* in full : all the reft *Chron.* The book of Pfalmes begins on Z 2 with a heading near the middle of the page, David playing on the harp.

The Apocrypha begin N n. 7, with a heading containing the creft of Walfingham, an old Elizabethan block. The New Teftament title reckons as Y y 4. It is remarkable for the mifprint TETSAMENT. The colophon is on K k k 8, recto. 1639. A variation has the N. T. title corrected, or fupplied from No. 155.

152.

Holy Bible.

Cambridge : T. Buck and R. Daniel.

4to. Black=letter. 1639.

The titles are plain.

153.

HOLY BIBLE.

London : Barker and affignes of Bill.

8vo. 1639-40-39.

The New Teft. title is dated 1640. The Colophon 1639. Probably the fame as No. 151 : the title page of 1640 being

prefixed to the New Teft. on account of the error (Tetfa-
ment) on the right one.

154.
Holy Bible.
London : Barker and Affignes of Bill.
Folio. Black-letter. 1640-39.

This is the laft of the great black-letter folio editions
which had commenced in 1611. It prefents few features
of difference from its predeceffors : except that being printed
with the fame type it has a generally faded and worn-out
look, efpecially at the corners where the lines furrounding
the page no longer meet, but gape apart. It may be re-
cognifed by having as the firft line of the dedication to King
James, the words, " To the Moft High," in capitals. The
New Teftament title is dated 1639. The marginal readings
are in Roman letter ; in the folios of 1611, 1613, 1617, and
1634 they were in Italics. As in 1634, the initial of Pfalm i.
has a cut of Cecil's arms.

155.
Holy Bible.
London : Barker and Affignes of Bill.
8vo. 1640-39.

New Teftament title 1639 : Colophon 1640. The Old
Teft. title is different from the title of the Bible of 1640.
There are 72 lines in a page. On verfo of the firft title the
royal arms and fupporters with C. R. Sometimes found
with the firft title of No. 158, or No. 159.

156.

𝕳𝖔𝖑𝖞 𝕭𝖎𝖇𝖑𝖊.

Cambridge: Buck and Daniel.   1640-39.

4to.   𝕭𝖑𝖆𝖈𝖐=𝖑𝖊𝖙𝖙𝖊𝖗.

A copy in Mr. Dix's Catalogue (Sotheby 1870) is faid
to have 1633 as the date of the New Teft. title.   1 Tim. iv.
16. Thy, *for* the.

157.

𝕳𝖔𝖑𝖞 𝕭𝖎𝖇𝖑𝖊.

London: Barker and Affigns of Bill.

4to.   𝕭𝖑𝖆𝖈𝖐=𝖑𝖊𝖙𝖙𝖊𝖗.   1640.

158.

HOLY BIBLE.

London: Barker and Affigns of Bill.

8vo.   1640.

The firft title differs from that of 1640-39-40, and has
a different fhield of arms on the verfo; no royal initials;
74 lines to a page. The New Teft. title may be diftinguifhed by having a large C. to the word commandement.
St. Matt. ix. 13. I not am come, *for* I am not come.

159.

HOLY BIBLE.

London: Barker and Affigns of Bill.

8vo.   1640.

On the New Teftament title commandement has a
fmall c.

160.

HOLY BIBLE.

London: Barker and Affignes of Bill.

12mo. 1640.

161.

NEW TESTAMENT.

London: Barker and Affigns of Bill.

12mo. fmall. 1640.

This edition and the fucceeding one are defcribed as 24mo. in the Britifh Mufeum Catalogue. The fignatures in both run in twelves. A 2—Y. 12. ends on verfo. No colophon. The title is on wood, with an arched defign, the 4 evangelifts, the facred name and other fymbols.

162.

NEW TESTAMENT.

London: Barker, &c. 1640.

12mo. fmall.

Differs little from preceding, has a border of conventional fleurs-de-lis round "Order of Books." The fignatures are the fame. Lea Wilfon (No. 80) defcribes a 32mo. of this date. Probably this.

163.

HOLY BIBLE.

London: Barker, &c. 1639-41.

12mo.

164.

𝕳oly 𝕭ible.

London: Barker, &c.   1640-41-42.

4to. 𝕭lack=letter.

The New Teftament title has 1641, and the colophon 1642.

165.

HOLY BIBLE.

London: Barker, &c.   1641.

8vo.

A variation is in the Britifh Mufeum.

166.

HOLY BIBLE.

London: Barker, &c.   1641.

12mo.

167.

𝕹ew 𝕿eftament.

London: Barker, &c.   1641.

8vo. 𝕭lack=letter.

Title, woodcut of an arch with emblematical figures and the four Evangelifts. The " names and order" on the verfo in a conventional border of fleurs-de-lis. Signatures A 2 to E e 8. verfo. Printed in long lines.

168.

HOLY BIBLE.

London: Barker and Affignes of Bill.

8vo.   1642.

There are three variations (Mr. Fry).

169.

HOLY BIBLE.

London: Barker, &c.   1642.

12mo.

A variety has 1643 New Teſt.

170.

NEW TESTAMENT.

London: Barker, &c.   1642.

12mo.

171.

HOLY BIBLE.

Edinburgh: Evan Tyler.   1642.

12mo.

172.

NEW TESTAMENT.

Edinburgh: R. Young and E. Tyler.

8vo.   1642.

I

173.

NEW TESTAMENT.

Edinburgh : Evan Tyler.   1642.
32mo.

174.

NEW TESTAMENT.

Edinburgh : James Bryſon.   1642.
12mo. ſmall, or 24mo.

"Edinburgh, printed by James Bryſon & are to be ſold at his ſhop a little above the Kirk ſtyle at yᵉ ſigne of the Golden Angel. An. Dom. 1642."

Mr. Ward has a copy of this Teſtament. Its ſize is 4 inches and an eighth by 1 and three-fourths.

175.

HOLY BIBLE.

Amſterdam : Printed by Jooſt Broerſs.
Folio.   1642.

This is apparently the firſt Engliſh Bible of the A. V. avowedly printed abroad. Jooſt Broerſs dwelt "in the Pije ſtreet, at the ſigne of the Printing houſe." The Genevan notes are added. Both titles engraved.

1 Tim. iv. 16, Thy, *for* the doctrine.

A variation has 1643 New Teſt.

176.

HOLY BIBLE.

London : Barker &c.   1643.
8vo.

There are at leaſt two varieties.

177.

HOLY BIBLE.
London : Barker &c. 1643.
12mo.

178.

NEW TESTAMENT.
London : Barker and Affignes of Bill.
12mo. 1643.

179.

New Teſtament.
Edinburgh : Evan Tyler. 1643.
8vo. Black-letter.

180.

NEW TESTAMENT.
Edinburgh : Evan Tyler. 1643.
32mo.

181.

HOLY BIBLE.
London : Printed in the yeere 1644.
8vo.
Royal arms on verſo of title. No line *Appointed*, &c.

182.

HOLY BIBLE.

    Amfterdam.   1644.

    Folio.

183.

HOLY BIBLE.

    Amfterdam : printed for C. P.   1644.

8vo.

Signatures run in 4 and four blanks, but are very irregular. In fize the book is fmaller than the ordinary fmall 12mo. of Field and others about this date. No line "Appointed &c." on either title-page. The numerals on the firft title, which has a woodcut border, are as follows:— CIƆ.ƆI.XLIV ; on the fecond, which is plain, M.D.C.XLIIII. No Apocrypha. Many contractions. New Teftament frefh fignatures A—Q (4.) verfo. No colophon. No chapter headings.

184.

HOLY BIBLE.

    London.   1644.

    12mo.

185.

HOLY BIBLE.

    Amfterdam :   printed   for   C.   P.

    ƆIƆ·ƆI·XLIV.   1644.

    12mo. or 24mo.

The fignatures run irregularly in fives and fevens ; Mr. Fry's copy meafures $2\frac{1}{4}$ inches by $4\frac{1}{2}$.

186.

HOLY BIBLE.

According to the copie printed for Roger Daniel, Printer to the Univerſitie of Cambridge.   1645.

4to.

1. Tim. iv. 16. Thy.

187.

HOLY BIBLE.

According to the copie, &c.   1645.

24mo.

This very ſcarce edition appears to have been printed like the foregoing at Amſterdam; it does not occur in the Britiſh Muſeum Catalogue.

188.

HOLY BIBLE.

Amſterdam : Joachim Noſche dwelling upon the Sea-dijck.   1645.

12mo. ſmall.

189.

HOLY BIBLE.

Roger Daniel, Printer to the Vniverſitie of Cambridge.   1645-46.

12mo.

On the title is a view labelled LONDVN.

190.

HOLY BIBLE.

London: Barker and Affignes of Bill.

8vo.   1646.

Title copperplate. The Royal Arms in a medallion and
a view of London Bridge. Lea Wilfon, No. 174.
Variation has the fecond date, 1648 (Mr. Fry).

191.

HOLY BIBLE.

London: William Bentley.   1646.

12mo.

Alluded to by Kilburne. See p. 35.

192.

NEW TESTAMENT.

London: Barker, &c.   1646.

12mo.

Mr. Fry has a Teftament of this date and name which
appears to belong to a complete Bible, and to have been
printed abroad.

193.

HOLY BIBLE.

London: Barker and Affignes of Bill.

8vo.   1647.

Three varieties. (Mr. Fry.)

194.

HOLY BIBLE.

London : Barker and Affignes of Bill.

12mo.   1647-54.

There are no Apocrypha though they are included in the lift. The New Teftament title has the name of Evan Tyler for a Society of Stationers, 1654. Col. fame.

195.

Holy Bible.

London : Thomas Brudenell and Robert White, for John Partridge.   1647.

12mo.   Black-letter.

Called by Lea Wilfon (176), 18mo. He adds " an extremely fmall and neat type." Very fcarce.

196.

New Teftament.

London : Barker and Affignes of Bill.

1647.

12mo. fmall, or 24mo.   Black-letter.

197.

NEW TESTAMENT.

Edinburgh : Evan Tyler.   1647.

16mo.

198.

New Testament.

Amfterdam : J. Canne.   1647.

12mo.

A copy was in Pickering's collection. It had the marginal notes known as Canne's.

199.

Holy Bible.

London : The Company of Stationers.

4to.   1648.

The title-page does not differ from that of Barker's quartos. The type is large. There are no Apocrypha.

200.

Holy Bible.

London : The Company of Stationers.

8vo.   1648.

201.

Holy Bible.

London : The Company of Stationers.

12mo.   1648.

Mr. Fry has five varieties.

202.

Holy Bible.

London : William Bentley.   1648.

8vo.

Alluded to by Kilburne, fee p. 35. Mr. Fry has two varieties.

203.

HOLY BIBLE.

London: John Field.   1648.

4to.

Mr. Fry has two editions of 1648. One of them has a
better engraved Title and no name to it. General defign
fame. Neither has any Apocrypha though they are mentioned in Names and Order. A third copy, imp. has
Apocrypha.

First title engraved by J. Payne: the fame plate as in
the folio of 1629, the 4to. of 1630, and feveral other Bibles.
See Nos. 72, 80, 81, 103, &c. No preface. The Apocrypha in fmaller type, apparently from another edition;
the fignatures are different and the pages numbered. Pfal.
cv. 29. and flew their flefh *for* fifh. N. T. title plain, with
a fmall woodcut of royal arms in the centre. 1 Tim. iv. 16.
Thy *for* the doctrine. New Teft. has frefh fignatures.
See under 1637.

204.

𝔑ew 𝔗eſtament.

London: Brudenell and White.   1648.

12mo. fmall.   𝔅lack-letter.

The fignatures run in five, and feven blank: Mr. Fry's
copy meafures two inches and a half by five and a half.

205.

HOLY BIBLE.

Cambridge: R. Daniel.   1648.

12mo.

206.

HOLY BIBLE.

Cambridge: Roger Daniel.   1648.

12mo. fmall, or 24mo.

The firft title, engraved, contains a view of London Bridge, very fimilar to that in Field's Bibles of 1657, &c. The imprint runs in a peculiar form which makes it difficult to fay whether this Bible was publifhed at Cambridge or in London : "Printed by Roger Daniel, printer to the Univerfitie of Cambridge," this name being in capitals: but below a fhield of the Royal Arms and over the London view is the word "London" alfo in capitals. Dedication A 2. recto. Names and order of Books verfo. Genefis begins A 3. Signatures run in ten and eight blank. The chapters have headings. The type is fair. No Apocrypha. New Teft. title comes as S 4. It has no border. Revelation ends on verfo A a 2 : no colophon. The texts ufually mifprinted in Acts vi. and 1. Tim. are here correct. See No. 189.

207.

NEW TESTAMENT.

Cambridge: R. Daniel.   1648.

12mo. fmall, or 24mo.

Mr. Francis Fry has fix copies apparently of this edition, which differ from one another in fome trifling particular.

208.

NEW TESTAMENT.

Edinburgh: E. Tyler.   1648.

8vo.

Double columns.

209.

HOLY BIBLE.

London : The Company of Stationers.

4to. 1649.

Large type : 50 lines to a full column. The title is within a heart-fhaped border, fimilar to that ufed for the Genevan and Barker's Bibles. Has the line " Appointed &c." Dedication on recto *A* 2. " The Tranflatours &c." Names and order on verfo. No preface. Text begins on B, ends on K k k k 8 recto. No Apocrypha. Malachi ends on P p p 4. No colophon. " FINIS."

This Bible is very correctly printed, avoiding the ufual errors at 1 Tim. iv. 16, and Acts vi. 3. It reads with Field's quarto of the previous year, but the error at Pfal. cv. 29 is corrected. (See No. 203.)

210.

HOLY BIBLE.

London : The Company of Stationers.

4to. 1649.

Title within ufual heartfhaped border. " The Holy Bible : containing the Old Teftament and the New : newly tranflated out of the originall Tongues : and with the former tranflations diligently compared and revifed : by his Majefties fpeciall commandment. *With moft profitable Annotations upon all the hard places, and other things of great importance :* which notes have never before been fet forth with this new Tranflation : *But are now placed in due order with great care and induftrie.* London ; printed by the Company of Stationers. 1649." Dedication *A* 2. Preface *A* 3, ending on *A* 5 verfo, 11 lines and a note. Then follow Names and

Order of Books; next the verſes uſual in Genevan Bibles, " Here is the ſpring whence waters flow ;" below which at the foot of the page is the collect, " O gracious God and moſt merciful Father, which haſt vouchſafed us the rich and precious Jewel, &c." The text begins on A 6. There are 74 lines in a full column. Malachi ends on S f verſo. There are no Apocrypha. The New Teſtament title differs little from that of the Old Teſtament, but has inſtead of the lines relating to the notes, theſe words, " With brief expoſitions of Theo. Beza upon the hard places, and the annotations of Fr. Junius upon the Revelation, &c." On the verſo of title is an addreſs from the printer to the Reader, and St. Matthew begins on recto A a a. Revelation ends on recto P p p 7. The Tables follow, on verſo, with continuous regiſter to verſo Q q q 8, on which page is a colophon :—
¶ Imprinted at London, by the Company of Stationers, 1649.

This Bible was purpoſely made to look as like the Genevan verſion as poſſible. Notes ſurround each page, and an " Argument" heads each book. The print is very ſmall, but clear.

In Offor's MS. Notes on the Genevan Bibles, (Brit. Mus. Addit. MSS. 26,672,) he calls attention to the republican doctrines put forward in the annotations upon Exod. i. 19 and 11 Chron. xv. 16. He alſo notes ſeveral errors:—

St. Luke xii. 47. And that ſervant which knew *not* his lord's will, *for* knew his lord's will.

St. John vii. 32. Fathers, *for* Phariſees.

Romans vii. 1. The firſt three ſyllables of " *domini*on" omitted. (Offor makes a miſtake himſelf, in his note on this verſe.)

11 Cor. vi. 4, 5. Faſtings *and* diſtreſſes, *tranſpoſed*.

1 Tim. iv. 16, Thy, *for* the.

211.

HOLY BIBLE.

London Company of Stationers. 1649.

12mo.

212.

HOLY BIBLE.

Edinburgh : Evan Tyler. 1649-50-55.

12mo.

On the New Teftament title, " London : Printed by the
Company of Stationers, 1650." Colophon, London, printed
by E. T. for a Society of Stationers, 1655." See No. 194.

213.

HOLY BIBLE.

Edinburgh : Evan Tyler. 1649.

8vo.

Dr. Lee (*Memorial*, p. 114) mentions this as the largeft
Bible printed by Tyler. A copy was in Daniel's collection ;
the New Teft. title dated 1648.

214.

HOLY BIBLE.

London : The Company of Stationers.

8vo. 1650.

Title within architectural cut, with David and the text
from the 51ft Pfalm, " Cor mundum crea in me Deus."
The king's arms in the tympanum of the arch, and on
the back of the firft title. Cut of Adam and Eve on A 3
above Genefis i. No Apocrypha. New Teft. title counts
M m 7. Colophon verfo of Z z 7.

215.

New Testament.

London: Company of Stationers. 1650.
16mo. Black-letter.

216.

Holy Bible.

London: Company of Stationers.

8vo.   1651-50.

New Teſtament title and colophon, 1650. Some have
col. 1655. A mixed and irregular edition.

217.

Holy Bible.

London: Companie of Stationers. 1651.

12mo.

Titles within the architectural woodcut. An open Bible
in the arch inſcribed *Verbum Dei.* No line "Appointed,
&c." No Apocrypha. New Teſt. title counts as D d 10.
No colophon. Revelation ends on verſo M m (12). 1 Tim.
5, numbered 10.

218.

Holy Bible.

London: Company of Stationers. 1652.

12mo.   A variety has N. T. title 1653.

219.

Holy Bible.

London: Field.   1653.

12mo.

Woodcut firſt title, very coarſely executed. Two ſhields,

one with a crofs, the other with a harp, above ; a view of
London Bridge below; the river has on it the word
" Thames." No Apocrypha. New Teſt. title ſimilar to
firſt. The colophon is on verſo Q q 6. This deſcription is
from Mr. Fry's copy; Mr. Ward has alſo one. A very
ſcarce edition.

220.
Holy Bible.

London: John Field, printer to the Parliament of England. 1653.

12mo.

Both titles engraved: the arms of the Commonwealth
at the top; London Bridge below.

221.
Holy Bible.

London : John Field. 1653.

12mo. ſmall, or 24mo.

Very incorrectly printed.

Old Teſtament title engraved : Moſes and David on each
ſide : The four Evangeliſts below: Juſtice and Mercy
above. No line "Appointed, &c." No Dedication or
Preface. Names and order, on verſo of title.

New Teſtament title, no date. Has line " Appointed
&c."

Lea Wilſon gives the following ſpecimens of the errors :

S. John ix. 21, Or who hath opened his eyes, *omitted.*

Romans vi. 13. Your members as inſtruments of righteouſneſs, *for* unrighteouſneſs.

1 Cor. vi. 9. The unrighteous ſhall inherit *for* ſhall not
inherit.

S. Matt. vi. 24. Ye cannot ferve and Mammon, GOD *omitted.*

S. John ii. 10. And when they have, *for* men have.

S. John iii. 21. Might be manifeft, *for* may be made manifeft.

This edition has the firft four Pfalms on the fame page. The above account is from Mr. F. Fry's copy.

222.

HOLY BIBLE.

London : John Field.   1653.

12mo. fmall, or 24mo.

Clofely refembles the preceding, but has fome of the errors correčted. Thofe in S. Matthew vi. 24, S. John ii. 10 ; iii. 21 ; ix. 21 ; and 1 Cor. vi. 9, remain. This edition does not read with the foregoing. Defcribed from Mr. Fry's copy. There are feveral other variations of this very incorrečt edition. They differ in the number of the errors, and in the fpelling and arrangement of the engraved title.

223.

HOLY BIBLE.

London : J. Field.   1653.

12mo. fmall, or 24mo.

A very correčt edition, clofely refembling the two preceding, but printed on thicker paper. It is faid by fome to have been printed abroad, but of this there is no direčt evidence. Pfalms 1, 2, and 3, on fame page.

Mr. Fry has a variation of this edition, differing flightly.

224.

HOLY BIBLE.

London : Field. 1653.

12mo. fmall or 24mo.

Only part of Pfalm i. on A a 4. In Mr. Fry's collection.

225.

HOLY BIBLE.

London : E. Tyler. 1653.

12mo.

This edition is often found with plates, clofely refembling thofe of the Scotch Bible of 1633.

226.

HOLY BIBLE.

London : Giles Calvert. 1653.

12mo. fmall.

Calvert was printer to many " Friends " and this has
been named the " Quakers' Bible." It is exceedingly fcarce :
the only perfect copy known being in the Baptift Library,
Stoke's Croft, Briftol.

Name and order of books on verfo of title : include the
Apocrypha. Malachi ends on verfo D d 6. There are
no Apocrypha and the regifter is continuous, the New Teft.
title counting as D d 7. Ends on verfo M m (10) high on
the page. *Finis :* no Col. Has the line " Appointed," &c.
Marginal notes.

K

227.

NEW TESTAMENT.
    London : Roger Daniel.   1653.
8vo. large.
    Scarce.

228.

NEW TESTAMENT.
    London : J. Flesher.   1653.
Folio.
    With a paraphrase and annotations by Henry Ham-
    mond. The First Edition. See No. 255.

229.

HOLY BIBLE.
    London : R. Daniel.   1654-53.
4to.
    Engraved O. T. title.

230.

HOLY BIBLE.
    London : R. Daniel.   1654.
4to.
    Lea Wilson No. 188. Acts vi. 3, whom ye, *for* whom
    we. Same plate as No. 229. for O. T. title.

231.

HOLY BIBLE.

London : Evan Tyler, for a Society of
Stationers. 1654.

12mo. ſmall.

Firſt title in a woodcut border. No line "Appointed"
&c. Names and order on verſo. Text begins A 2. No
Apocrypha. Signatures run in ſix and ſix blank. No
chapter headings. New Teſt. title ſimilar to firſt title.
No line "Appointed &c." Counts as Q q 6. Texts in
1 Tim. iv. and Acts vi. correct ; but general typography
irregular and bad. Ends on verſo D d d (12): no colophon.

232.

HOLY BIBLE.

London : E. T. for Stationers. 1655.

4to.

Woodcut title, heart ſhaped.

233.

HOLY BIBLE.

London : E. T. for a Society of Stationers.

8vo. 1655.

This Bible is one of the few printed during the Commonwealth which contains neither the uſual error in Acts vi.
3, nor that in 1 Tim. iv. 16. But *Epitle* is printed for
Epiſtle on Y y 1. Sig. P p 3 miſprinted H p 3. V v is miſprinted V u and V v 3, V u 3.

234.

HOLY BIBLE.

London : Evan Tyler, for a Society of
Stationers.   1655.

12mo.

235.

HOLY BIBLE.

London : Field.   1655.

8vo.

236.

HOLY BIBLE.

London : John Field, one of His High-
nes's printers.   1655.

12mo. fmall.

"Of this book Kilburne fays, 'In a fmall bible in
volume 12°. printed by John Field at London in 1655,
whereof great numbers have been difperfed, a catalogue of
91 notorious faults, amongft many others therein . . one
whereof is 11 Cor. xiii. 6, . . which is wholly omitted.'
The book fully juftifies the complaint."—*L. Wilfon*,
p. 117.

Engraved title.   1 Tim. iv. 16, Thy, *for* the.

237.

HOLY BIBLE.

London : Field.   1656-55.

Engraved title refembling that of No. 221.

ttt

238.

HOLY BIBLE.

London: John Field.　　1656.

12mo.

239.

New Teſtament.

London: J. Streater.　　1656.

16mo. **Black-letter.**

This Teſtament counts as an 8vo. The Finis is on verſo
X x 8.

240.

HOLY BIBLE.

London: John Feild.　　1657-55.

12mo.

New Teſt. title and Colophon dated 1655, and printer's
name correctly ſpelt. This is a very incorrect edition.
Iſa. xxviii. 17, overthrow, *for* overflow. St. Luke xxiii. 43.
them *for* him. Romans vi. 13. righteouſneſs *for* unrighteouſneſs. Some of the miſprints are mentioned by *Kilburne*
(See p. 41), but this edition has evidently been corrected to
a certain extent.

241.

HOLY BIBLE.

London: John Feild.　　1657-56.

12mo.

New Teſt. title and colophon 1656. 1 Tim. iv. 16,

Thy. Firſt title engraved by Vaughan. The miſſpelling of the printer's name does not occur on the N. T. title, which is plain. No line " Appointed &c." on either.

242.

HOLY BIBLE.

London : Field.   1657-56.

12mo. ſmall or 24mo.

243.

HOLY BIBLE.

London : Field.   1657.

12mo.

Probably the ſame as No. 241. " Very incorrect, but typography good."—L. W. 192.

244.

HOLY BIBLE.

London : Field.   1657.

18mo.

" Groſſly incorrect, and printed with a battered, worn-out type."—L. W. 193. Probably ſame as No. 242.

245.

HOLY BIBLE.

London : Roger Daniel cɔɔclvij.   1657.

8vo.

No Apocrypha. No colophon. Has uſually a ſeries of engravings on copper.

Acts vi. 3. Whom ye, *for* whom we.
1 Tim. iv. 16. Thy doctrine, *for* the doctrine.
S. Matt. i. 16. Wo, *for* who.
S. Matt. xiii. 14. Wayfaid, *for* wayfide.

246.

HOLY BIBLE.
London : James Flefher. 1657.
12mo.

Very correctly printed. Scarce.

247.

HOLY BIBLE.
Cambridge : John Field, printer to the
Vniverfitie. 1657.
8vo.

Of this edition Kilburne fays, " In another minion-
bible in 8vo. volume printed by John Field at Cambridge
in 1657, which fells very much and very dear, at leaft for
8*s*. 6*d*. per book, Pfalm cxliii. 4, ' *Therefore is my fpirit
over*,' is wholly omitted in many of them that I have feen."
This Pfalm begins on recto T t 7. Acts vi. 3, *whom ye
may appoint.* The Pfalmes in Meeter, which follow, have
a continuous regifter. In a variation (Mr. Fry) the error
at Pfa. cxliii. is corrected.
There is a different iffue in which Pfalm cxliii, begins
on verfo T t 6, and is correct.

248.

HOLY BIBLE.

London : Hills and Field.   1657-58.

12mo.

Firſt title engraved by P. Lombart.   No line " Appointed."   Col. 1658.

249.

HOLY BIBLE.

Cambridge : Field.   1657-61.

8vo.

Engraved title by Vaughan.   New Teſt. title 1661.

250.

HOLY BIBLE.

London : J. Field, " one of His Highnefs's Printers."   1658.

12mo. ſmall, or 24mo.

Exceedingly incorrect.   The title is engraved with a view
of London Bridge, above which are two ſhields, one charged
with *a croſs, ſable;* the other which is enſigned with a crown,
has a *plain croſs, couped* : in the centre the Royal Arms, with
a crown and within a garter.   The title, which wants the
line *Appointed* &c., is on a tablet, ſupported by Moſes and
Aaron.   Above on a broken pediment is an open Bible,
" John cap. j. ver. 17. *The law was given by Moſes, but
grace and truth came by* Jeſus Chriſt."   This edition has no

border round New Teft. title, which alfo wants the line
" Appointed &c."

The pfalms begin on Y 12. verfo.

Jeremiah ii. 26. Chief, *for* thief.

Philip. iii. 17. Of or enfample, *for* for an enfample.

II. Thefs. ii. 5. Whom I was, *for* when I was.

II. Thefs. ii. 15. Paul faft, *for* ftand faft.

A variation is corrected by the infertion of the line
" Appointed." There are feveral other varieties which
read together and differ chiefly in the fpelling, and arrangement of the titles.

251.

HOLY BIBLE.

London : John Field. 1658.

12mo. fmall, or 24mo.

The New Teft. title has a border, but the line " Appointed " &c., is not on either title. Does not read with
the foregoing.

Pfalms begin on A a 12 recto.

Jer. ii. 26. Chief, *for* thief.

Ifaiah liii. *heading* Jefaiah.

Another varies only in having the line " Appointed,"
on the firft title.

252.

HOLY BIBLE.

Cambridge : John Field. 1659.

Folio.

This is the fame edition as that of the following year
which is embellifhed with Ogilby's engravings, except that
the Old Teftament titles differ.

Acts vi. 3. Ye *for* we. 1 Tim. iv. 16. Thy *for* the.

253.
NEW TESTAMENT.

London : Jeremiah Rich.   1659.
64mo.   In short-hand.

254.
NEW TESTAMENT.

London : E. Tyler.   1659.
12mo.   *Italics.*

With Beza's latin version in parallel columns, and a preface of 8 pages signed *Charles Hoole.*

255.
NEW TESTAMENT.

London.   1659.
Folio.

With Hammond's paraphrase and notes. Dr. Cotton mentions this as the second edition, a third in 16(71), a fourth in 1675, a fifth in 1681, a sixth in 1689, and a seventh, which Lowndes calls the best, folio, London 1702. See No. 228.

256.
HOLY BIBLE.

Cambridge : Printed by John Field, printer to the Universitie, and illustrated with Chorographical Sculps. by J. Ogilby.

Folio.   1660-59.

Does not differ from No. 252, except in the first title and in the plates by Ogilby.

Old Teft. title engraved; " Solomon on his throne," drawn by *Diepenbeck*, engraved by *Lombart*. New Teft. title very plain, dated 1659. Separate regifter to New Teftament. No Apocrypha. Colophon 1659. Type very diftinct.

Acts vi. 3. Ye *for* we. 1 Tim. iv. 16. Thy *for* the.

This Bible exceeds in fize even the folio of 1611. Lea Wilfon's copy is defcribed as on large paper, but it is probable there were none on fmaller paper. The inconvenient fize of the volume is noticed by *Pepys*, 27th May, 1667.

257.

HOLY BIBLE.

London : Henry Hills and John Field.

Square 8vo. or fmall 4to. 1660.

Titles very plain. No colophon. No apocrypha. 1 Tim. iv. 16. Thy *for* the.

Some copies have firft title engraved, and the name of Henry Hills only.

258.

HOLY BIBLE.

London : John Field. 1660.

8vo.

Signatures count in twelves.

259.

HOLY BIBLE.

London : John Feild. 1660.

12mo.

Firft title engraved by Vaughan. The fpelling of the printer's name is fometimes correct. Acts vi. 3. Ye *for* we. 1 Tim. iv. 16. Thy *for* the.

260.

NEW TESTAMENT.

London : Jer. Rich.   1660.

64mo.   In ſhort-hand.

261.

HOLY BIBLE.

Cambridge : John Field.   1660.

8vo.

Noticed in *Horne*, vol. v. p. 100.   Acts vi. 3. Ye *for* we.

262.

HOLY BIBLE.

London : John Bill and Chriſtopher
Barker.   1661-60.

12mo.

New Teſt. Title, London : John Field, 1660. Both titles
plain. No line " Appointed," &c. on either. The apocrypha with ſeparate ſignatures and in ſmaller print : not
mentioned in names and order of books : probably an
inſertion. The Prophets end on verſo K k 11 ; New
Teſt. title counts as K k 12, and S. Matt. begins on L l (1).
Revelation ends verſo V v 11. Colophon, " John Field,
1660." Acts vi. 3, Whom ye may appoint, *for* whom we.
1 Tim. iv. 16. Thy *for* the doctrine.

Another, with the ſame dates, has the firſt title engraved by Vaughan, with Field's name.

263.

HOLY BIBLE.

London: Chriſtopher Barker. 1661.

4to.

The Old Teſt. title is engraved by P. Williamſon.
King David in the foreground and text from Pſa. li. The
New Teſtament title and the colophon read, *London, printed
by Henry Hills.* There is a freſh regiſter for the New Teſt.
which has a handſome cut of the King's arms on the title.
Apocrypha begin G g g. 1 Tim. iv. 16. Thy.

A variation in Mr. Fry's collection has a printed firſt
title with the names of J. Bill and C. Barker.

264.

HOLY BIBLE.

Cambridge: J. Field. 1661.

8vo.

Engraved firſt title. Acts vi. 3. Whom ye, *for* whom we.
1 Tim. iv. 16. Thy *for* the.

265.

NEW TESTAMENT.

Cambridge: J. Field. 1661.

8vo.

Acts vi. 3. Ye *for* we. 1 Tim. iv. 16. Thy *for* the.

266.

HOLY BIBLE.

Cambridge : J. Field.   1661-62.

8vo.

Paged 1-965, O. T. and 1-299, N. T., p. 965 numbered
985. No line " Appointed " on either title. Firſt title
engraved. No Apocrypha. Aĉts vi. 3. Ye. 1 Tim. iv.
16. Thy.

267.

HOLY BIBLE.

(Amſterdam ?)   1662.

12mo.

With Canne's notes. Probably printed by Swart or
ſome other Dutch printer. The titles are printed with
borders of acorns. There is no printer's name or place.
The names and order of books is on verſo firſt title. Then
follows on A 2 an addreſs " To the Reader," ſigned on
verſo, " John Canne." No dedication. Geneſis begins A.
Prophets end verſo L l (11). New Teſt. title counts as
L l 12. St. Matt. begins M m (1). Revelation ends verſo
Y y 4. 1 Tim. iv. 16. Thy doĉtrine.

268.

NEW TESTAMENT.

Cambridge : Field.   1662.

8vo.

Aĉts vi. 3. Ye. 1 Tim. iv. 16. Thy.

269.

HOLY BIBLE.

Cambridge : Field.   1663.

4to.

A variation has 1662, New Teſt. title.

270.

HOLY BIBLE.

London : Bill and Barker.   1663.

8vo.

> Engraved title. Portions of this and the next often occur mixed in the fame volume.

271.

HOLY BIBLE.

Cambridge : Field.   1663.

8vo.
> Engraved title.

272.

HOLY BIBLE.

Printed Anno 1664.

Large 12mo.

> Woodcut firft title : defign very fingular; a fpread eagle occupies the greater part. No Apocrypha. Probably printed at Amfterdam.

273.

HOLY BIBLE.

John Field, " printer to the Uneverfete of Cambrig."   1664.

12mo.

> The firft title, engraved, has the ufual view of London. New Teft. title, " printed in the Yeare 1664."

274.

New Testament.
        London : Bill and Barker.   1664.
    12mo.

275.

Holy Bible.
        London : Bill and Barker.   1665-62.
    12mo.

276.

Holy Bible.
        London : J. Bill and C. Barker.   1665.
    8vo.
        The apocrypha in fmaller type.
        Acts vi. 3. Ye *for* we. 1 Tim. iv. 16. Thy *for* the.
        A fcarce edition.

277.

Holy Bible.
        London : J. Bill and C. Barker.   1666.
    12mo.
        Acts vi. 3, Ye. 1 Tim. iv. 16, Thy. Defcribed by
    L. Wifon (202) as an 18mo.

278.

Holy Bible.
        Cambridge : Field.   1666.
    4to.
                1 Tim. iv. 16, Thy.

279.

HOLY BIBLE.

Cambridge: Field. 1668-66.

4to. Small type.

This edition is known as Field's *Preaching Bible*. It was well adapted for the pulpit. The firſt title is engraved. The New Teſt. title is dated 1666. The New Teſt. has a diſtinÆt regiſter. No Apocrypha.

280.

HOLY BIBLE.

London : Bill and Barker. 1668.

12mo.

The Apocrypha are included in the liſt.

281.

HOLY BIBLE.

Cambridge: Field. 1668.

4to.

1 Tim. iv. 16. Thy *for* the doÆtrine.

282.

HOLY BIBLE.

London : Bill and Barker. 1669.

8vo.

Firſt title engraved ; ſometimes illuſtrated with engrav-

L

ings by Van Have. New Teſt. title printed, "In the Savoy," by the affigns of Bill and Barker. There is a variation, which differs but flightly. Both have 1 Tim. iv. 16, Thy.

283.

HOLY BIBLE.

> London : Bill and Barker.   1669.

12mo.

> *Note in Lea Wilſon*, No. 204 :—" Apparently printed abroad."

284.

NEW TESTAMENT.

> Edinburgh ; George Swinton and James Glen.   1669.

12mo. (?)

> Dr. Lee (*Memorials*, p. 116) mentions this edition. It is in the Roman letter.

285.

HOLY BIBLE.

> London : Bill and Barker.   1670.

8vo.

286.

HOLY BIBLE.

> London : Bill and Barker.   1670.

12mo.

287.

New Testament.

Edinburgh : Andro Anderson. 1670.

12mo. **Black-letter.**

Mentioned by *Lee*, p. 116. Is there a copy extant?

288.

HOLY BIBLE.

Cambridge : John Hayes. 1670.

4to.

Engraved Title. 1 Tim. iv. 16. Thy, *for* the. One of the B. M. copies is entered as 8vo.

289.

New Testament.

Glasgow : Robert Sanders, printer to the Town, and are to be sold in his Shop.

12mo. **Black-letter.** 1670.

Probably the first Glasgow Testament. Acts vi. 3. Ye.

290.

HOLY BIBLE.

London : Bill and Barker. 1670-71.

8vo.

291.

HOLY BIBLE.

London : Bill and Barker. 1670-75.

8vo.

292.

HOLY BIBLE.

London: Bill and Barker.   1671-69.

8vo.

New Teſtament 1669. 1 Tim. iv. 16. Thy. New
Teſt. title. In the Savoy, Aſſigns of Bill and Barker, 1669.
Differs from the edition of 1669 in fig. Zz, the heading of
St. James i.

293.

HOLY BIBLE.

London: Bill and Barker.   1671-69.

8vo.

The title differs from the foregoing as does the Old
Teſtament ; the New Teſt. dated 1669 is the ſame as that
of the Bible of 1669.

294.

HOLY BIBLE.

London: Bill and Barker.   1671.

8vo.

Firſt title copper-plate ; architectural pattern. On a
broken pediment an angel blowing a trumpet. Dedication
A(1). Names and order on verſo. No Apocrypha. Prophets
end verſo P p p 2. New Teſtament title, plain, within
black lines, counts as P p p 3. " In the Savoy," Aſſigns of
Bill and Barker, 1671. Revelation ends verſo K k k k (8).
No colophon. Acts vi. 3. Ye may, *for* we may. 1 Tim.
iv. 16. Thy doctrine, *for* the. Ezek. xl. *headed* Ezeliel
Chap. xi. Proverbs i. headed Chap. V.

295.

HOLY BIBLE.
London: Affigns of Bill and Barker.
12mo.   1672.

296.

New Teſtament.
Glaſgow: Sanders.   1672.
12mo. **Black-letter.**

Lowndes, p. 236A. Acts vi. 3. Ye.

297.

HOLY BIBLE.
Amſterdam: Stephen Swart, bookſeller
near the Exchange.   1672.
Folio.

1 Tim. iv. 16. Thy. With Canne's notes.
Some copies have no printer's name on either title.
Others have an engraved firſt title with view of London.

298.

HOLY BIBLE.
London: Bill and Barker.   1672-73.
12mo. ſmall, or 24mo.

299.

HOLY BIBLE.

London : R. Barker and Affigns of Bill.
12mo.   1673.

300.

HOLY BIBLE.

London : Robert Barker.   1673.
12mo.

301.

HOLY BIBLE.

London : Affigns of J. Bill and C.
Barker.   1673.
12mo.

302.

HOLY BIBLE.

Cambridge : John Hayes.   1673.
4to.

1 Tim. iv. 16. Thy, *for* the. Ephefians ii. 13. Sometime, *inftead of* fometimes, as it is ufually erroneoufly printed.

303.

HOLY BIBLE.

Edinburgh : Andrew Anderfon.   1673.
12mo.

Acts vi. 3. Ye may, *for* we may. With notes, fee *Lee*, p. 128. *Lewis* (p. 340) calls this an 8vo.

304.

HOLY BIBLE.

Edinburgh : Anderſon. 1673.

18mo.

" In a letter called pereill letter," ſee Lee, *Memorial*,
p. 128.

305.

HOLY BIBLE.

London : Aſſigns of Bill, &c. 1674-73.

12mo.

306.

HOLY BIBLE.

London : Bill and Barker. 1674.

12mo.

307.

HOLY BIBLE.

London : Aſſngs of Bill and Barker.

24mo. 1674.

Lea Wilſon, No. 209. Acts vi. 3. Ye may, *for* we may.

308.

NEW TESTAMENT.

London : Aſſigns of Bill and Barker.

12mo. 1674.

309.

New Testament.
London: Affigns of Bill and Barker.
12mo. Black-letter.   1674.
Double Columns.

310.

HOLY BIBLE.
Cambridge: J. Hayes.   1674.
Folio.
1 Tim. iv. 16. Thy.   Engraved title.

311.

HOLY BIBLE.
Oxford: At the Theater.   1675-73.
4to.

The New Teft. title dated 1675, the colophon 1673.
The firft Bible printed at Oxford. The general title engraved reprefenting the Transfiguration. Acrofs the centre
is a label, "The Holy Bible." A mount bears "Mᵗ.
Tabor, Matt. xvii. 1." In the foreground are two feated
female figures. One is veiled and has underneath the
words, "The Law." The other has a nimbus and is
infcribed "The Gofpel." On the bafe of a broken column
to the left is "At the Theater in Oxon. No date. This
is followed by a printed title, 1675. Names of books on
verfo. Text begins A (1). Prophets end verfo C c (4).
Apocrypha begin (A) in fmaller type; end verfo (I 3).

New Teftament title engraved. An obelifk on which an angel writes, with an arrow, " The Law of Loue from the Hill of Sion." On the bafe is infcribed " The Law of Fear from Mount Sinai." Three fmall angels above fupport a label " The New Teftament." Below, on a ftep, is written, At the Theater in Oxford Aº 1675. This plate is followed by a printed title, 1675. St. Matt. begins (A). Revelation ends verfo (P 7). Colophon, " At the Theater in Oxford, MDCLXXIII." 1 Tim. iv. 16. Thy doctrine, *for* the.

Mr. Fry has a variation in which the colophon is dated 1675.

312.

HOLY BIBLE.
 London : Affigns of Bill and Barker.
8vo.   1675.

313.

HOLY BIBLE.
 London : Affigns of Bill and Barker.
12mo.   1675.

314.

HOLY BIBLE.
 Cambridge : Hayes.   1675.
4to.
      1 Tim. iv. 16. Thy.

315.

Holy Bible.
Edinburgh : Andrew Anderfon.
12mo. 1675.

316.

New Testament.
Edinburgh : Andrew Anderfon. 1675.
12mo.

Called 18mo. in Lea Wilfon, and 8vo. by *Lewis*, p.
340. Acts vi. 3. Ye may, *for* we may.

317.

Holy Bible.
London : Bill and Barker. 1676-75.
8vo.

Firft title engraved. Apocrypha in lift. New Teft. title,
1675. 1 Tim. iv. 16. Thy.

318.

Holy Bible.
London : Bill and Barker. 1676.
8vo.

319.

HOLY BIBLE.

London : Affigns of Bill and Barker.

12mo., fmall, or 24mo. 1676.

Acts vi. 3. Ye may appoint. 1 Tim. iv. 16. Thy
doctrine. Mr. Fry has two varieties.

320.

HOLY BIBLE.

London : C. Barker. 1676.

4to.

Probably printed in Holland. Scarce. 1 Tim. iv. 16.
Thy doctrine.

321.

NEW TESTAMENT.

London: Bill and Barker. 1676.

8vo.

Headings in Black-letter. Title plain. No colophon.
Acts vi. 3. Ye, *for* we. 1 Tim. iv. 16. Thy, *for* the.
Sometimes defcribed as 12mo.

322.

HOLY BIBLE.

Edinburgh : Andrew Anderfon. Printer
to his moft Sacred Majefty, King Charles
the Second, in the 28 year of his reign.

8vo. 1676.

" In a letter called non-pereill," with notes ; *Lee,* p. 128.
1 Tim. iv. 16. Thy doctrine. Dr. Lee, p. 163, praifes
this edition as the beft of its fize and period.

323.

HOLY BIBLE.
　Cambridge : Hayes.　　　1677-75.
4to.

324.

HOLY BIBLE.
　London : Bill and Barker.　1677-76.
4to.

325.

HOLY BIBLE.
　London : Bill and Barker.　　1677.
12mo.

326.

NEW TESTAMENT.
　London, in the Savoy : Bill and Barker.
8vo.　　　　　　　　　　　1677.
　Acts vi. 3. Ye may.　1 Tim. iv. 16. Thy doctrine.

327.

HOLY BIBLE.
　Cambridge : J. Hayes.　　　1677.
4to.
　With additional parallel texts.　1 Tim. iv. 16. Thy.

328.

HOLY BIBLE.

Edinburgh : heirs of Anderſon.

12mo.   1678-73.

The New Teſtament is dated " R. Barker and Aſſignes of J. Bill, 1673." It is ſcarce : a copy was in Mr. Dix's collection. It is probably one of thoſe alluded to by Dr. Lee.

329.

HOLY BIBLE.

London : Bill, Barker, Newcomb and Hills.   1678.

4to.

Firſt title engraved.   Has uſually a printed title to follow the engraving.

1 Tim. iv. 16. Thy.

330.

HOLY BIBLE.

London : Bill and Barker.   1678.

4to.   A different edition.

331.

HOLY BIBLE.

London :   Bill &c.   1678.

12mo.

332.

New Testament.
London: Bill &c.   1678.
12mo.   Black-letter.

333.

HOLY BIBLE.
Edinburgh: Heirs of Anderſon.   1678.
4to.
Mentioned with commendation by Dr. Lee, p. 163.

334.

HOLY BIBLE.
Oxford: at the Theater.   1679-75.
4to.
New Teſt. dated 1675.

335.

HOLY BIBLE.
London: Bill, Newcomb, and Hills.
8vo.   1679.
Aɛts vi. 3. Ye may.   1 Tim. iv. 16. Thy.

336.

HOLY BIBLE.
London: Bill, Newcomb, and Hills.
8vo.   1679.
Another edition.

337.
HOLY BIBLE.

London: Bill, Barker, Newcomb and Hills. 1679.

12mo.

338.
New Testament.

London: Bill and Newcomb. 1679.

12mo. Black-letter.

339.
New Testament.

Newcomb and Hills. 1679.

8vo. Black-letter.

A&s vi. 3. Ye. 1 Tim. iv. 16. Thy.

340.
HOLY BIBLE.

Oxford: At the Theater. 1679.

Sm. 4to.

Title engraved.

There is no New Teft. title: this is the cafe with feveral Oxford Bibles. Apocrypha in flightly fmaller type, with frefh fignatures. Dedication on A 1. No preface. Names and order of books, on verfo of Dedication. Frefh fignatures in the New Teftament. 1 Tim. iv. 16. Thy, *for* the.

Colophon:—" Printed at the Theater in Oxford, and are to be fold by Mofes Pitt at the Angel in St. Paul's church-yard, Peter Parker at the Leg and Star, over againft the Exchange in Cornhill, Thomas Guy at the Corner of Little Lumbard Street, and William Leak at the Crown in Fleet Street. London, Anno 1679."

Some copies are illuftrated with " The Holy Bible in Sculpture; London, Mofes Pitt at the Angel in St. Paul's churchyard, 1683 :" the title of which, engraved on copper, follows the engraved general title of the Bible.

341.

HOLY BIBLE.

> Oxford : At the Theater.   1679.
> 4to.

Alfo publifhed in London. Varies but little from the foregoing.

342.

NEW TESTAMENT.

> Oxford : At the Theater.   1679.
> 8vo.

343.

HOLY BIBLE.

> Amfterdam : S. Swart, " at the Crowned Bible on the Weft fide of the Exchange."
> Folio.   1679.

Ufually embellifhed with plates. Acts vi. 3. Ye. 1 Tim. iv. 16. Thy.

344.

HOLY BIBLE.

No place or printer's name. 1679.

Folio.

The fame edition, flightly varied. On the engraved title-page is a view of London Bridge.

A copy of this edition is in the Library of Edinburgh Univerfity, and in the accounts there is an entry relating to it, by which it appears that " 18 lib." was the price. See Dr. Lee, p. 12, *lift*.

345.

NEW TESTAMENT.

No place or printer's name. 1679.

12mo.

This is poffibly a Scottifh edition ; it is alfo attributed to Amfterdam.

346.

New Teſtament.

Printed 1679.

16mo. Black-letter.

Very fcarce. Acts vi. 3. Ye may appoint, *for* we may. 1 Tim. iv. 16. Thy, *for* the. The fignatures, which are very irregular, generally run in 5 and 3 blanks. There is no place or printer's name. The text is in double columns. The page meafures, in Mr. Ward's copy, $6\frac{1}{4}$ inches by $3\frac{3}{4}$ Probably printed at Glafgow.

M

347.

HOLY BIBLE.

London : Bill and Barker. 1680-69.

8vo.

New Teftament dated 1669.

348.

HOLY BIBLE.

London : Bill and Barker. 1680-75.

8vo.

New Teftament dated 1675.

349.

HOLY BIBLE.

London : Bill and Barker. 1680.

8vo.

350.

HOLY BIBLE.

London : Bill and Barker. 1680.

12mo.

Title in a rude woodcut; imitated from the ufual architectural pattern. No line "Appointed, &c." Paper very
coarfe. The print large and clear. Malachy ends on verfo
D d 3. New Teftament title plain; line "Appointed, &c."
Counts as D d 4. Sig. M m contains fix leaves. Revelation ends verfo M m 6. No colophon.

351.
NEW TESTAMENT.
London: Bill, Newcomb, and Hills.
8vo.   1680.

Lowndes, p. 2634.

352.
NEW TESTAMENT.
Cambridge: J. Hayes.   1680.
4to.

1 Tim. iv. 16. Thy.

353.
HOLY BIBLE.
Oxford: Theater.   1680.
Folio.

Very large. Both titles engraved. Colophon has the names of Pitt, Parker, Leake, and Guy. 1 Tim. iv. 16. Thy.

354.
HOLY BIBLE.
Oxford: Theater.   1680.
8vo.

Publiſhed in London. Engraved title. Acts vi. 3. Ye may, *for* we may.

355.

HOLY BIBLE.

Oxford : Theater,

8vo. 1680-81.

For Thomas Guy, London.

356.

HOLY BIBLE.

Oxford : Theater. 1680-82.

Small 8vo.

New Teſt. dated 1682.

357.

HOLY BIBLE.

London : Bill, Hills, and Newcomb.

12mo. ſmall. 1680-84.

Acts vi. 3. Ye. 1 Tim. iv. 16. Thy.

358.

HOLY BIBLE.

London : Bill &c. 1681.

12mo.

Titles printed.

359.

HOLY BIBLE.

London : Bill &c. 1681.

12mo. fmall, or 24mo.

Acts vi. 3. Ye. 1 Tim. iv. 16. Thy.

360.

NEW TESTAMENT.

London : Bill &c. 1681.

12mo. fmall, or 24mo.

361.

HOLY BIBLE.

Oxford : Theater for Peter Parker at the Leg and Star, Cornhill. (1681 ?) Folio.

No date. No New Teft. title. Old Teft. title engraved. Placed under 1681, in Brit. Mus. Catalogue. Small folio, half the fize of No. 351.

362.

HOLY BIBLE.

Oxford : Theater for T. Guy.

12mo. large. 1681.

New Teft. title has the names of Leake, Parker, &c. Acts vi. 3. Ye. 1 Tim. iv. 16. Thy.

363.

Holy Bible.

    Cambridge : Field.   1682-1666.

4to.

    One of the preaching Bibles : fee under 1668-66.

364.

Holy Bible.

    London : Affigns of Bill &c.   1682-75.

8vo.

365.

Holy Bible.

    Cambridge : J. Hayes.   1682-80.

4to.

366.

Holy Bible.

    London : Affigns of Bill, and by New-
comb and Hills.   1682.

8vo.

    Acts vi. 3. Ye. 1 Tim. iv. 16. Thy.

367.

Holy Bible.

    London : Bill, Newcomb, and Hills.

12mo.   1682.

    Engraved firft title. Very inaccurate. The following
examples will fuffice, as every page has its errata :—

Genefis ix. 5. At the hand of man, *omitted*.

Genefis xxi. 26. Neither didft thou tell me, *omitted*.

Genefis xxx. 35. And all the brown among the fheep, *omitted*.

Deut. xxiv. 3. If the latter hufband ate her, *for* hate her.

Efther vi. 2 kings, *for* keepers.

Jeremiah xiii. 27. adverfaries *for* adulteries.

Jerem. xvi. 6. glad *for* bald.

Jer. xviii. 21. fwine, *for* famine.

Ezek. xviii. 25. The way of the Lord is equal, *for* not equal.

The ufual error alfo occurs at 1 Tim. iv. 16.

A number of italic letters are interfperfed with the text, efpecially at the beginning (Gen. iii. 24, 25; xiv. 27, 35, &c.) : They probably refer to notes which were afterwards withdrawn, the reference letter being carelefly left. Probably printed at Amfterdam with a fictitious title.

368.

HOLY BIBLE.

Cambridge : John Hayes. 1682.

4to.

The Apocrypha are in the lift of books.

369.

HOLY BIBLE.

Oxford : Theater. 1682.

Folio.

There are feveral variations of this edition. The Britifh Mufeum has one which bears on the firft title the words, " Are to be fold by Ann Leake over againft Dean St. in Fetter Lane, London, 1682." The New Teft. title has the names of Mofes Pitt, William Leake, and Thomas Guy.

Mr. Francis Fry's copy has on the firft title the name of Peter Parker " at the Leg and Star, over againft the Royal Exchange."

The fame volume fometimes occurs without any New Teft. title, and this may be faid of almoft all the Oxford Bibles. Several will be found hereinafter noticed of which the New Teft. title, if it ever exifted, is not now to be found.

370.

HOLY BIBLE.

Oxford: Theater, for Ann Leake. 1682. 4to.

No N. T. title.

371.

HOLY BIBLE.

Oxford: Theater.   1682. 8vo.

The firft title, which is engraved, bears no date. The fignatures are very irregular, but generally count as in a 16mo.

372.

HOLY BIBLE.

Oxford: Theater, for T. Guy.   1682. 8vo.

Differs from the foregoing. Firft title alfo engraved and without date.

373.

HOLY BIBLE.

No place or printer's name. 1682.

12mo.

Firſt title engraved on wood.

374.

HOLY BIBLE.

(No place or printer's name.) 1682.

12mo.

With Canne's notes. Probably printed in Holland, but
ſometimes attributed to the Edinburgh preſs. Very incor-
reɛt: e. g. Ezek. xviii. 25. The way of the Lord is equal,
for not equal. 1 Tim. iv. 16. Thy, *for* the.

375.

HOLY BIBLE.

London : Aſſigns of Bill and Barker.

12mo. 1682-84.

New Teſt. title, 1684.

376.

HOLY BIBLE.

Cambridge : J. Hayes. 1683-66.

4to.

Firſt title engraved. New Teſt. title has the name of
John Field, Cambridge, and the date 1666. 1 Tim. iv.
16, Thy, *for* the.

377.

HOLY BIBLE.

Cambridge : J. Hayes.   1683-80.

4to.

General title engraved.   Dedication A 1.   No preface.
Apocrypha with ſeparate regiſter.   New Teſt. title printed ;
date 1680.   Separate regiſter.   No colophon.   1 Tim. iv.
16.   Thy, *for* the.

378.

HOLY BIBLE.

London : Aſſigns of Bill and Barker.
8vo.   1683.

379.

HOLY BIBLE.

London : Aſſigns of Bill, Hills and
Newcome.   1683.

12mo.

Firſt title engraved.

380.

NEW TESTAMENT.

London : Bill, Hills, and Newcomb.
8vo.   1683.

381.

HOLY BIBLE.

    Cambridge: J. Hayes.   1683.

4to.

    This is an edition of the flat Preaching Bible.

382.

HOLY BIBLE.

    Cambridge: J. Hayes.   1683.

4to.

    General title engraved. Apocrypha have a diſtinct re-
giſter beginning A. New Teſt. title printed : New Teſt.
freſh regiſter beginning A.

383.

HOLY BIBLE.

    Oxford: at the Theater; for Moſes Pitt,
Peter Parker, Thomas Guy and Ann Leake.

    4to.   1683.

    General title engraved: undated. 1 Tim. iv. 16.
Thy, *for* the.

384.

HOLY BIBLE.

    No place or printer's name.   1683.

Folio.

    With Genevan notes. Probably printed by Swartz or

his widow, at Amfterdam. Nicholaus Viffcher's name
occurs on the maps by which it is ufually illuftrated. Acts
vi. 3, whom ye may appoint. 1 Tim. iv. 16, Thy doctrine.
There are two general titles, one of them engraved. The
Apocrypha have a diftinct regifter.

385.
NEW TESTAMENT.
London: for Thomas Simmons.   1683.
4to.
With Clark's annotations. This firft edition is fcarce.

386.
HOLY BIBLE.
London: Affings of J. Bill, T. Newcomb
and H. Hills.   1684.
12mo.
Entered in the B. M. Catalogue as an 8vo. It differs
from the next Bible in being printed on thicker paper and
in having the error at S. John i. corrected. The error on
the Old Teftament title remains. 1 Tim. iv. 16. Thy
doctrine. Probably printed at Amfterdam.

387.
HOLY BIBLE.
London: Affings of J. Bill, Thomas
Newcomb and Henry Hills.   1684.
12mo.
This is a fpurious edition, printed probably at Amfter-

dam. At the commencement of St. John's Gofpel the heading of the page is S. Jean, *for* S. John. 1 Tim. iv. 16. Thy, *for* the.

The title-pages are very plain. The New Teft. title is correctly fpelt. No Apocrypha. Genefis begins on A 2. New Teft. title counts E e (1.)

388.
HOLY BIBLE.

London : Affings of Bill &c.   1684.

12mo.

Refembles preceding, but has Canne's preface and notes. Scarce. Probably with the two foregoing, printed at Amfterdam.

389.
HOLY BIBLE.

London : Affigns of J. Bill, T. Newcomb and H. Hills.   1684.

12mo. fmall.

The New Teft. title has the names in a different order, "Bill, Hills & Newcomb." Mr. Francis Fry has two other editions of this date and fize, one of which refembles the above, but is not of the fame fetting up : the other has the name of C. Bill for that of J. Bill.

390.
HOLY BIBLE.

Oxford : Theater, for Thomas Guy.
1684.

Folio.

The general title is engraved. Apocrypha in lift.

There is no title to the New Teftament. S. Matthew
begins on ¶ A. Scarce; does not occur in Lowndes, Lea
Wilfon, or the Britifh Mufeum Catalogue : nor was it in
Offor's or Pickering's colle&tions. Mr. Francis Fry has a
copy, and another is in the colle&tion of Archdeacon Harrifon at Canterbury Cathedral.

391.

NEW TESTAMENT.
    Amfterdam : Widow of Steven Swart.

                                       1684.
12mo.

392.

NEW TESTAMENT.
    Amfterdam : Widow of Steven Swart.

                                       1684.
12mo.

    With the Dutch and French verfions in parallel columns.

393.

HOLY BIBLE.
    London : Affigns of Bill, Hills and New-
comb.   1684-85.
    12mo. fmall, or 24mo.

    N. T. title, 1685.

394.

HOLY BIBLE.

London: Affigns of Bill, Hills, and
Newcomb.   1685.

4to.

395.

HOLY BIBLE.

London: Affigns of Bill and Newcomb.

1685.

8vo.

Mentioned by Horne, vol. v. p. 100. Acts vi. 3, Ye
for we.

396.

HOLY BIBLE.

London: Affigns of Bill, Hills and
Newcomb.   1685.

12mo.

The Apocrypha are named in the lift of books.

397.

NEW TESTAMENT.

London: B. Simmons.   1685.

4to.

With Richard Baxter's paraphrafe and notes: among
this is one on 1 Tim. iv. 16, in which the erroneous reading
Thy *for* the is adopted.

398.

HOLY BIBLE.

Oxford : Theater.   1685.

8vo. ſmall.

Engraved general title.   No New Teſt. title.   S. Matt.
begins Ddddd.

399.

HOLY BIBLE.

Oxford : Theater, " and now to be Sold
by Thomas Guy, at the Oxford Arms in
Lombard Street, near Pope's Head Alley."

1685.

12mo.

No New Teſt. title.

400.

HOLY BIBLE.

Oxford : Theater.   1685.

Folio.

401.

HOLY BIBLE.

London : R. Roberts.   1685.

Folio, 2 vols.

The publication of this Bible, which has annotations
and various readings, was commenced in 1683, by Matthew
Poole, a Diſſenter, and continued after his death.

402.

HOLY BIBLE.

Oxford : Theater, for Thomas Guy.

1685-86.

12mo.

403.

HOLY BIBLE.

Oxford : Theater, for Guy.   1685-86.

12mo. ſmall.

404.

HOLY BIBLE.

London : Bill, Hills and Newcomb.

1686.

12mo.

The Apocrypha are included in the Names and order of the Books, but are not in the volume. The Prophets end on Sig. F f. recto, which ſhould be F f 4. and St. Matt. begins on F f 6. verſo of F f 4 being blank, and New Teſt. title counting as F f 5.   Both titles without borders.

Revelation ends on verſo O o 12.   No colophon.

Acts vi. 3. whom ye may appoint, *for* whom we.

1 *Tim.* iv. 16. Thy doctrine, *for* the.

405.

NEW TESTAMENT.

London : Bill, Hills, and Newcomb.

8vo.   1686.

N

406.

Holy Bible.

Oxford : Theater, for Peter Parker.

4to.   1686.

Both titles engraved.

407.

Holy Bible.

Oxford : Theater, for Guy.   1686.

8vo. ſmall.

408.

Holy Bible.

Oxford : Theater.   1686.

12mo.

No New Teſt. title. Acts vi. 3, ye may appoint.
1 Tim. iv. 16, Thy doctrine.

409.

New Teſtament

Glaſgow : Robert Sanders.   1686.

12mo.   Black-letter.

410.

Holy Bible.

Oxford : Theater, for T. Guy.

12mo.   1686-87.

The laſt page of Revelation is filled up with a table of
kindred.

411.

Holy Bible.

Oxford : Theater, for T. Guy.

4to.   1687-86.

412.

Holy Bible.

London : C. Bill, H. Hills, T. Newcomb.   1687.

12mo.

413.

Holy Bible.

London : W. Addy.   1687.

16mo. in fhorthand.

Engraved by J. Sturt.   There are two editions of this
date and fize.

414.

Holy Bible.

Oxford : Printed at the Theater in Oxford, & are to be fold by Thomas Guy at
the Oxford Arms on the Weft fide of the
Royal Exchange in Cornhill.   1687.

12mo.
             No New Teft. title.

415.

HOLY BIBLE.

Oxford: Theater: for Guy.   1688-82.
4to.

416.

HOLY BIBLE.

London: C. Bill, H. Hills, and T.
Newcomb.   1688.

12mo.

The Apocryphal Books are named in the lift, but the
fignatures run on without them.

417.

HOLY BIBLE.

London: R. Roberts.   1688.
Folio, two vols.

Poole's Bible: this edition was commenced in 1685.

418.

HOLY BIBLE.

Oxford : Theater: for Thomas Guy.
Folio, fmall.   1688.

Columns divided by a double line. Large woodcut of
Royal arms on firft title. Smaller cut on New Teft. title
with initials J. R. Has the Apocrypha with a continuous
regifter. Mr. T. M. Ward has a copy.

419.

HOLY BIBLE.

Oxford : Theater : for Peter Parker.

Folio, fmall. 1688

Differs from the foregoing only in the titles.

420.

HOLY BIBLE.

Oxford : Theater. 1688.

12mo. fmall.

421.

HOLY BIBLE.

Oxford : Theater. 1688.

4to.

422.

HOLY BIBLE.

London : Affigns of Bill, Newcomb and Hills. 1689.

12mo.

New Teftament title, " Affings." Apparently printed abroad. Firft title within an architectural border : names of books on verfo. Text A 2.—D d 3 verfo, " Malachy." The fame fig. repeated Matt. i. New Teft. title plain. No line " Appointed &c." on firft title. Ends on verfo of M m 6. No colophon. Correctly printed, but on coarfe paper. Some copies have a different N. T. title dated 1669.

423.

HOLY BIBLE.

Oxford : Theater.   1689.

8vo.

Acts vi. 3. Ye may. 1 Tim. iv. 16. Thy, *for* the.

424.

HOLY BIBLE.

London : Bill and Newcomb.   1690.

8vo.

425.

HOLY BIBLE.

London : J. Heptinftall.   1690.

Folio.

With annotations &c. by S. Clark.

426.

HOLY BIBLE.

London : Chifwell and Robinfon, and
Aylmer.   1690.

Folio.

The fame edition, but with different publifher's name.

427.

HOLY BIBLE.

London : C. Bill and Thomas Newcomb.

12mo.   1691.

Meafures 6 inches by 3½.

428.

Holy Bible.

London : C. Bill and Executrix of J. Newcomb.　　1691.

12mo. ſmall.

Mr. Francis Fry's copy 4¾ inches by 2½. Has the Apocrypha in the liſt of books.

429.

New Teſtament.

London : Bill and Newcomb.　　1691.

8vo.　Black=letter.

Plain printed title. Names and order of books on verſo. Text begins A 2, ends x 6 verſo, top of page. " Finis," no colophon. Double columns. 1 Tim. iv. 16. Thy.

430.

Holy Bible.

Oxford : Theater : for T. Guy.　　1691.

12mo.

Printed titles.

431.

Holy Bible.

Oxford : Theater : for T. Guy.　　1691.

12mo. ſmall.

Printed titles. Mr. F. Fry's copy meaſures 5½ by 3 inches. Acts vi. 3. whom ye may, *for* we. 1 Tim. iv. 16. Thy doctrine, *for* the. A variation has Peter Parker's name on titles.

432.
New Testament.

Glafgow : Robert Sanders.   1691.

12mo. Black-letter.

Acts vi. 3. Whom ye may appoint. Generally very
incorrectly printed.

433.
HOLY BIBLE.

Oxford : Theater.   1692.

12mo.

434.
HOLY BIBLE.

London : C. Bill and T. Newcomb.

12mo. fmall.   1693-91.

The firft title is engraved : it has the name of T. Newcomb on it, although he muft have died in 1691. The New
Teft. title is dated 1691.

435.
HOLY BIBLE.

London : Printed by Charles Bill and the
Executrix of Thomas Newcomb, deceas'd,
printers to the King and Queen's moft Excellent Majefties.   1693.

4to.

436.

HOLY BIBLE.

London : C. Bill and Ex^x T. Newcomb.
8vo.   1694.

Mr. Francis Fry has an imperfect Bible with this date
on the New Teft. title. I have not been able to find a perfect copy.

437.

HOLY BIBLE.

London : C. Bill, &c.   1694.
12mo.

438.

HOLY BIBLE.

Edinburgh : Printed by the Heir and
fucceffors of Andrew Anderfon.   1694.
12mo.

Scarce. 1 Tim. iv. 16. Thy, *for* the.

439.

𝔑ew 𝔗eftament.

Edinburgh : Printed by the Heirs and
Succeffors of Andrew Anderfon, Printer to
their moft Excellent Majefties.   1694.
12mo. 𝔅lack=letter.

This edition is called " fpurious" in the Britiſh Muſeum catalogue. Dr. Lee accepts it as genuine. A note-book is attached to the Britiſh Muſeum copy in which upwards of 400 errors are enumerated. Many are omitted in the liſt and ſome added by miſtake. The following ſelection has been verified :—

S. Matt. ii. 18, Rame, *for* Ramah.

S. Matt. vii. 3, brackers, *for* brother's.

S. Matt. vii. 27. the houſe, *for* that houſe.

S. Matt. viii. *heading*, chapter ix.

S. Matt. viii. 12, dardneſs, *for* darkneſs.

S. Matt. viii. 27, obey them, *for* obey him.

S. Matt. xiii. 41, them which do do iniquity.

S. Matt. xxii. 15, when, *for* went.

S. Matt. xxvii. 20, and, *for* aſk.

S. Mark i. *heading* chapter ii.

S. Mark ii. 18, the diſciples of John and of John.

S. Mark vii. 35, eyes, *for* ears.

S. Mark vii. 36, 37, *numbered* 26, 27.

S. Luke ii. 36, ſeventy years, *for* ſeven.

S. Luke viii. 35, her right mind, *for* his.

S. Luke xxiii. 47, this man was, *for* this was.

S. Luke xxiv. *heading* 14.

S. John v. 32, knoweth, *for* I know.

S. John vi. 49, your father, *for* your fathers.

S. John vii. 31, peole, *for* people.

S. John ix. 26, Then ſaid they to him again, *repeated*.

S. John x. 3, leadeth them not, *for* out.

Acts ii. 6, ſpeaking, *for* ſpeak in.

Acts x. 23, longed, *for* lodged.

Acts x. *heading* 11.

Acts xi. 11, There, *for* three.

Acts xii. 21, otion, *for* oration.

Acts xiii. 23, accorning, *for* according.

Acts xiv. 8, ma, *for* man.

Acts xviii. *headed* xxvii.
Acts xx. 3, spira, *for* Syria.
Acts xxiv. 24, Prifcilla, *for* Drufilla.
Acts xxvi. 14, beaking, *for* fpeaking.
Romans ix. *heading* x.
Romans viii. 32, forgive, *for* give.
1 Cor. ix. *heading* x.
1 Cor. ix. 1, feen Jefus, *for* not feen
1 Cor. xiii. 4, wanteth, *for* vaunteth.
II Cor. x. 14, preached, *for* reached.
II Thefs. i. 9, publifhed, *for* punifhed.
II Tim. iv. 4, tears, *for* ears.
II Tim. iv. 16, with ftood, *for* ftood with.
Titus, *heading*, Tius.
S. James v. 20, which covereth the finner, *for* converteth.
1 S. Peter iii. 11, fpeak, *for* feek.
Rev. xiv. verfes 16, 17, 18, *omitted.*
Rev. xiv. verfes 19, 20, *numbered* 17, 18.

It would be very fafe to affert that every column has one or more miftakes. There is no fign that this Teftament was not really printed in Edinburgh. The paper is very coarfe and bad.

440.

HOLY BIBLE.
London: C. Bill and Ex^x of T. Newcomb.
12mo. 1695.

The Apocrypha are named in the lift of books, but the fignatures run without them.

441.

HOLY BIBLE.

London : Addy.   1695.

16mo. fhorthand.

Engraved by Sturt.

442.

NEW TESTAMENT.

London : T. Parkhurft, &c.   1695.

8vo.

With Baxter's commentary. Second edition. 1 Tim.
iv. 16, Thy, *for* the. The fame reading is adopted in the
note. See No. 393.

443.

HOLY BIBLE.

Oxford : Printed by the Univerfity
printers.   1695.

12mo.

Lea Wilfon calls this an 18mo. 1 Tim. iv. 16, Thy.
S. Luke xi. *numbered* xii.

444.

HOLY BIBLE.

London : C. Bill, &c.   1696.

Folio.

445.
HOLY BIBLE.
    London : C. Bill, &c.   1696.
  12mo.

446.
NEW TESTAMENT.
    London : C. Bill, &c.   1696.
  8vo.

447.
New Teſtament.
    London : C. Bill, &c.   1696.
  16mo. Black-letter.

448.
HOLY BIBLE.
    Oxford : Univerſity Preſs.   1696.
  12mo. ſmall.

449.
HOLY BIBLE.
    Edinburgh : Heirs of Anderſon.   1696.
  12mo.
      Called an 18mo. in Lea Wilſon. Has Canne's notes.

450.

HOLY BIBLE.

London: C. Bill, &c.   1697.

12mo.

451.

HOLY BIBLE.

London: C. Bill, &c.   1697.

4to.

No Apocrypha. No colophon. 1 Tim. iv. 16, thy *for* the. There is ufually an engraved title dated 1678, prefixed.

452.

HOLY BIBLE.

Oxford: Univerfity Prefs.   1697.

4to.

Engraved title by M. Burghers. The Apocrypha included in the lift of books.

453.

HOLY BIBLE.

London: C. Bill, &c.

12mo. fmall.   1698-96.

New Teft. title dated 1696. Firft title engraved: the arms of William III. fupported by angels, being in front.

454.

Holy Bible.

London : C. Bill, &c. 1698.

12mo.

With Canne's notes. 1 Tim. iv. 16, Thy, *for* the.

455.

Holy Bible.

Edinburgh : Heirs of Anderfon. 1698.

12mo. fmall.

Lea Wilfon, 227. Lee (p. 164) fays this edition " is not only indiftinctly printed but full of errors. It would be difagreeable to point them out minutely : but the following fpecimen is taken almoft at random. Mark iii. 26, againft Satan, *for* againft himfelf : Luke i. 31, bring for, *for* bring forth : John i. 13, of the flefh, *for* of the will of the flefh : Romans ii. 13, does of the law, *for* doers of the law : Romans vi. 17, ye were not the fervants of fin, *for* ye were the fervants of fin : Romans viii. 33, eject, *for* elect."

456.

Holy Bible.

London : C. Bill, &c.

12mo. fmall. 1698-99.

Mr. Francis Fry's copy meafures 5 inches by $2\frac{1}{2}$. New Teft. title 1699. There is a variation diftinguifhed only by having an engraved title.

457.

Holy Bible.
      London : C. Bill, &c.   1698-1700.
   12mo. fmall.

458.

Holy Bible.
      London : C. Bill, &c.   1699.
   8vo.
                        Engraved title.

459.

Holy Bible.
      London : C. Bill, &c.   1699.
   12mo.

460.

Holy Bible.
      Oxford : Univerfity.   1699.
   12mo.

461.

Holy Bible.
      Oxford : Univerfity.   1699.
   24mo.
                  1 Tim. iv. 16. Thy.

462.

NEW TESTAMENT.

Oxford : Univerſity. 1699.
12mo. ſmall.

Called 24mo. in Lea Wilſon.

463.

HOLY BIBLE.

Edinburgh : Heirs of Anderſon.
4to. 1700-1699.

New Teſtament 1699. No Apocrypha. 1 Tim. iv. 16,
Thy doctrine, *for* the doctrine.

464.

HOLY BIBLE.

London : C. Bill, &c. 1700.
4to.

With Canne's notes. 1 Tim. iv. 16, Thy, *for* the. Said
to have been printed abroad. The firſt title engraved :
figure of King David: two pillars and an arch, in the head
of which are the royal arms. The ſame arms are in woodcut on New Teſt. title. They are obſervable as being thoſe
of William III., but without the ineſcutcheon for Naſſau.
The initials W. R. are on the New Teſt. title. No Apocrypha. Canne's preface and no dedication.

465.

HOLY BIBLE.

London : C. Bill, &c. 1700.
12mo.

466.

New Testament.

London : Bill and Ex^r. of Newcomb.

12mo.   1700.

467.

Holy Bible.

London : (printed at Amfterdam).   1700.
4to.

With Canne's notes.

468.

New Testament.

Amfterdam : widow of S. Swart.   1700.
12mo.

Acts vi. 3, Ye may, *for* we may.   1 Tim. iv. 16, Thy,
for the.   With the Dutch verfion, in parallel columns.

469.

New Testament.

Amfterdam : widow of S. Swart.   1700.
12mo.

Acts vi. 3, Ye may, *for* we may.   1 Tim. iv. 16, Thy.
With the French verfion, in parallel columns.

470.
New Testament.
   London: Rich.   1700.
32mo. fhorthand.

   With portrait of Rich. Twentieth impreffion.

471.
Holy Bible.
   London.   1700.
Folio.

   With Poole's annotations: beft edition. 1 Tim. iv. 16.
Thy, *for* the.

472.
New Testament.
   Leyden: Van der May.   1700.

   Mentioned, with doubt, by Cotton, p. 80, *note*.

473.
Holy Bible.
   London: C. Bill, &c.   1701.
Folio.

   Engraved title, reprefenting a Gothic cathedral, by B.
Lans, engraved by Sturt: index. Apocrypha. No colophon.
A printed title follows the engraving, with a woodcut of
the arms of William III. and the motto, " Je main tien

dray." Dedication, a and verſo. Preface, a 2—a (6) reſto.
verſo, Names and order of Books. Text begins on A (1)
with a woodcut initial, repreſenting Adam and Eve. The
Chronology is given at the upper corner, with the Julian
Period, Cycle of the Sun, Dominical Letter, &c. Prophets
end Q q q (6) reſto, paged 743. Verſo blank. Apocrypha
R r r (1.) page 745. End G g g g 8. Verſo, page 916.
New Teſt. title reſembles ſecond title Old Teſt. and counts
as H h h h (1). Text begins H h h h 2, page 919: ends,
reſto C c c c c (6.) verſo. Tables of Affinity, &c. An index
follows with freſh ſignatures, but referred to by a catchword
(" An ") at foot of Tables. 1 Tim. iv. 16. Thy, *for* the.
This Bible differs entirely from the edition of the ſame date
and ſize ſuperintended at Oxford by Dr. Lloyd.

474.

Holy Bible.
Oxford : Univerſity.   1701.
Folio.

Dates and index by Biſhop Lloyd.   No pagination.
Each part diſtinſt regiſter.   Apocrypha in ſmaller type.
Engraved title, preceding printed one.   Signatures of text,
A.—G g g 4.   Next two leaves blank.   Then H h h, one
leaf blank and I i i alone.   Prophets ending on verſo.
Apocrypha begin on a, end on reſto (S 2.) a blank leaf.
New Teſt. title engraved by Burghers : repreſents St. John
in Patmos.   Printed title follows.   Text A 2—verſo R (6).
Followed by an index with ſeparate ſignatures.   The chro-
nology is given at heads of the columns throughout the
book.   1 Tim. iv. 16. Thy, *for* the.

475.

HOLY BIBLE.

London: Bill, &c. 1702.

4to.

Firſt title engraved. Initial Gen. i. "Adam and Eve."
1 Tim. iv. 16. Thy, *for* the.

476.

HOLY BIBLE.

London: Bill, &c. 1702.

12mo.

Engraved title.

477.

HOLY BIBLE.

London : Bill, &c. 1702.

24mo.

1 Tim. iv. 16. Thy, *for* the.

478.

HOLY BIBLE.

London: Bill, &c. 1703-02.

8vo.

New Teſtament 1702.

479.

HOLY BIBLE.

London: Bill, &c. 1703.

Folio.

480.

HOLY BIBLE.
    London : Bill, &c.   1703.
4to.

481.

HOLY BIBLE.
    London : Bill, &c.   1703.
8vo.

    Both titles engraved.

482.

HOLY BIBLE.
    London : Bill, &c.   1703.
12mo.
    The Apocrypha are included in the lift of Books.

483.

HOLY BIBLE.
    Oxford : Univerfity.   1703.
4to.

484.

HOLY BIBLE.
    London : Bill, &c.   1703-04.
12mo.
            New Teftament 1704.

485.

HOLY BIBLE.
London : Bill, &c.   1703-07.
8vo.

1 Tim. iv. 16, Thy.

486.

HOLY BIBLE.
London : Bill, &c.   1704.
12mo.

487.

𝔑ew 𝔗eſtament.
London : Bill, &c.   1704.
8vo. ſmall. 𝔅lack=letter.

1 Tim. iv. 16. Thy, *for* the.   Probably printed abroad.

488.

NEW TESTAMENT.
London : Bill, &c.   1704.
8vo.

489.

𝔑ew 𝔗eſtament.
London : Bill, &c.   1704.
12mo. 𝔅lack=letter.

Probably printed in Holland, like No. 487.

490.

HOLY BIBLE.
     Oxford: Univerſity.   1704.
I 2mo.

     Called 18mo. by Lea Wilſon.   The ſize is 5 × 2½ inches.

491.

HOLY BIBLE.
     London: Bill and Executrix of New-
comb.   1705.
     I 2mo.

         I Tim. iv. 16. Thy, *for* the.

492.

NEW TESTAMENT.
     London: Bill, &c.   1705.
I 2mo.

493.

HOLY BIBLE.
     Oxford: Univerſity.   1705.
8vo.

494.
Holy Bible.

Edinburgh : Heirs of Anderſon.   1705.
4to.

Very badly printed.   For ſpecimen ſee Lee's *Memorial*,
p. 167.

495.
Holy Bible.

Edinburgh : Heirs of Anderſon.   1705.
12mo.

Very incorrectly printed, according to *Lee, p.* 166.

496.
Holy Bible.

London: C. Bill and Executrix of Thomas
Newcomb.   1706.
Folio, ſmall.

Engraved title, ſimilar to that of 1701 : followed by
printed title. Apocrypha with continuous regiſter. 1 Tim.
iv. 16. Thy, *for* the. Tables and index, commencing at
foot of laſt page of Revelation : T t t t 4. recto.—X x x x 6.
recto.

497.
Holy Bible.

London: Bill, &c.   1706.
4to.

498.

HOLY BIBLE.
     London: Bill, &c.   1706.
    12mo. fmall.

499.

HOLY BIBLE.
     Oxford: Univerfity.   1706.
    4to.

500.

HOLY BIBLE.
     Oxford: Univerfity.   1706.
    12mo.

501.

NEW TESTAMENT.
     Oxford: Univerfity.   1706.
    4to.

502.

HOLY BIBLE.
     London: Bill and Executrix of New-
comb.   1707.
    12mo.

    This Bible was really printed by Mrs. Anderfon at
Edinburgh. The woodcut border of the title contains the
arms of Scotland and thofe of the city of Edinburgh. See
for defcription and *facfimile* Dr. Lee's *Memorial*, p. 161.

503.
HOLY BIBLE.
    Oxford : Univerſity.   1707.
    12mo. ſmall.
        Mr. Fry's copy meaſures 4½ inches by 2½.

504.
HOLY BIBLE.
    London : Bill, &c.   1708-06.
    12mo.

505.
HOLY BIBLE.
    London : Bill, &c.   1708-07.
    12mo.

506.
HOLY BIBLE.
    No place : (Amſterdam).   1708-07.
    Folio.
        With Genevan notes. Firſt title engraved with view of
    London. 1 Tim. iv. 16. Thy, *for* the. New Teſtament
    dated 1707.

507.
HOLY BIBLE.
    (Amſterdam).   1708.
    Folio.
        Genevan notes : engraved title with view of London.
    1 Tim. iv. 16. Thy.

508.

HOLY BIBLE.
    London: C. Bill, &c.   1708.
4to.

509.

HOLY BIBLE.
    London: C. Bill, &c.   1708.
4to.
            With the Apocrypha.

510.

HOLY BIBLE.
    London: C. Bill, &c.   1708.
8vo.

511.

HOLY BIBLE.
    Oxford: Univerſity.   1708.
12mo. ſmall.
        Mr. Fry's copy meaſures 5 inches by 2½.

512.

HOLY BIBLE.

London : C. Bill, &c.   1709.

Folio.

> 1 Tim. iv. 16. Thy, *for* the.   This appears to be the laſt folio Bible printed by the repreſentatives of Chriſtopher Barker, or Barkar, who had obtained the patent as Royal Printer in 1577.   Thomas Baſkett purchaſed the remaining thirty years of Newcomb and Bill's patent in 1709.   In 1769 Charles Eyre bought Baſkett's patent, and at the preſent date, 1872, Meſſrs. Eyre and Spottiſwoode continue a ſucceſſion which has been unbroken ſince 1565.   See p. 11, &c. in the Introductory notice : and a paſſage in Dr. Lee's *Memorial*, p. 179.

513.

NEW TESTAMENT.

London : C. Bill, &c.   1709.

8vo.

> The headline is in 𝔅𝔩𝔞𝔠𝔨-𝔩𝔢𝔱𝔱𝔢𝔯.   Mr. Francis Fry has a copy.   Scarce.

514.

HOLY BIBLE.

Oxford : Univerſity.   1709.

4to.

> With the Apocrypha and an Index.

515.
Holy Bible.
London : Affigns of Newcomb & Hills.
8vo.   1710.

516.
Holy Bible.
London : Affigns of Newcomb & Hills.
12mo.   1710.

517.
New Testament.
London : Bill, &c.   1710.
12mo. fmall.

   1 Tim. iv. 16. Thy, *for* the.

518.
Holy Bible.
Edinburgh : Heirs of Andrew Anderfon.
12mo.   1710.

519.
Holy Bible.
London : Affigns of Newcomb & Hills.
Folio.   1710-11.

  Named in Pickering's Catalogue, III. No. 1628.

520.

HOLY BIBLE.

London : Affigns of Thomas Newcomb
& Henry Hills, deceafed, Printers to the
Queen.   1711-10.

12mo.

New Teft. title 1710. Lea Wilfon calls this an 18mo.
His copy is in the Britifh Mufeum. It is very erroneoufly
printed, *e.g.* St. John x. 28, neither fhall any pluck, *for* any
man pluck. St. John x. 29, And none, *for* no man.

521.

HOLY BIBLE.

London : Affigns of Newcomb & Hills.
8vo.   1711.

522.

HOLY BIBLE.

London : Affigns of Newcomb & Hills.
12mo. fmall.   1711.

523.

HOLY BIBLE.

Oxford : Univerfity.   1711.
8vo.

Ifaiah lvii. 12. I will declare thy righteoufnefs and thy
works, for they fhall profit thee, *for* fhall not profit thee.

524.

HOLY BIBLE.

Oxford : Univerſity.   1711.

12mo.

There were probably at leaſt two editions of this ſize and year.

525.

HOLY BIBLE.

London : Aſſigns of Thomas Newcomb and Henry Hills, deceaſed.   1711-12.

8vo.

The New Teſtament title bears the names of John Baſkett and the aſſigns of T. Newcomb and Henry Hills.   1712.

Appendix.

P

Lift of the Bibles of the Authorifed Verfion in the Library of the Britifh Mufeum: from 1611 to 1711.

T HE following lift was copied from the Catalogue, in 1871, duplicates being omitted. Although in many cafes the fize is erroneoufly given or is determined by fome ftandard with which I am unacquainted, I have thought it beft not to make any alteration. The reference number to my own lift will help the reader to determine the edition.

1611. folio, copperplate title: (3050 g. 1.) firft
     iffue, B. L.   I

  „   „ woodcut title: (3050 g. 2.) fecond
     iffue, B. L.   2

  „   „ with reprints, B. L.   .   .

1612. 4to. (imperfect, wanting A 7.) .   .   .   4

  „ 8vo. (Another, clofely cut, is called 12mo.
     in Catalogue)   5

		No.
1628. 8vo.	. . . . .	63
1628. 4to. 𝕭. 𝕷.	. . . . .	62
1629. 12mo. London	. . . .	71
,, folio, London	. . . .	68
,, folio, Cambridge	. . . .	72
,, folio, Cambridge, printed only on one fide, wants Old Teſt.	. . . .	72
1630. 4to. Cambridge	. . . .	80
,, 4to. Cambridge, 𝕭. 𝕷.	. . .	81
,, 4to. London	. . . .	75
,, 4to. London, 𝕭. 𝕷.	. . .	73
,, 4to. London (another Edition) 𝕭. 𝕷.	.	74
,, 8vo. London	. . . .	77
1631-30. 8vo. London	. . . .	83
1631. 8vo. London	. . . .	84
,, 8vo. London	. . . .	85
1632-31. 4to. London, 𝕭. 𝕷.	. . .	91
1632. folio, London	. . .	93
,, 8vo. London	. . .	95
1633-32. folio, London	. . .	97
1633. 4to. London	. . . .	98
1633. 8vo. Edinburgh	. . .	104
,, 12mo. London	. . .	100
1634. 8vo. London	. . . .	111
,, folio, London, 𝕭. 𝕷.	. . .	109
,, 4to. London, 𝕭. 𝕷.	. .	110
1635. 4to. Cambridge, 𝕭. 𝕷.	. .	118
,, 12mo. London	. .	115
1636. 4to. London	. . . .	122
1637. 4to. Cambridge	. . .	130
,, 4to. Cambridge. 𝕭. 𝕷.	. .	131

		No.
1646. 12mo. London	. . . . .	191
1647. 8vo. London .	. . . .	193
„ 12mo. London, 𝔅. 𝕷.	. . .	195
1648. 4to. London .	. . . .	199
„ 4to. London .	. . . .	203
„ 8vo. London .	. . . .	200
„ 12mo. Cambridge .	. . .	205
„ 12mo. London	. . . .	201
„ 18mo. Cambridge .	. . .	206
„ 36mo. Cambridge .	. . .	206
1649-48. 8vo. Edinburgh	. . .	213
1649. 4to. London .	. . . .	209
1650. 8vo. London .	. . . .	214
1651-50. 8vo. London	. . . .	216
1651. 12mo. London	. . . .	217
1653. 12mo. London	. . . .	219
„ 12mo. London	. . . .	225
„ 12mo. London	. . . .	221
„ 24mo. London	. . . .	223
1654-53. 4to. London	. . .	229
1654. 12mo. London	. . . .	231
1655. 8vo. London	. . . .	233
„ 8vo. London .	. . . .	235
„ 12mo. London	. . . .	234
„ 12mo. London	. . . .	236
1657-55. 12mo. London	. . .	240
1657-56. 12mo. London .	. . .	241
1657. 12mo. London	. . . .	246
„ 8vo. Cambridge	. . . .	247
1658. 12mo. London	. . . .	250
„ 12mo. London	. . . .	251

List of Bibles.

217

	No.
1675. 12mo. London	313
1676-75. 8vo. London	317
1676. 8vo. Edinburgh	322
„ 12mo. London	319
1677-76. 4to. London	324
1677. 12mo. London	325
1678. 4to. London	329
„ 12mo. London	331
1679. folio	344
„ 4to. Oxford	340
„ 4to. Oxford	341
„ 8vo. London	335
„ 8vo. London	336
1680. folio, Oxford	353
„ 8vo. Oxford	354
„ 12mo. London	350
1681. folio, Oxford	361
„ 12mo. London	358
„ 24mo. London	359
1682-75. 8vo. London	364
1682. folio, Oxford	369
„ 4to. Oxford	370
„ 12mo. London	367
1682-84. 12mo. London	375
1682. 12mo.	374
1683. 12mo. London	379
„ 4to. Oxford	383
„ folio	384
1683-66. 4to. Cambridge	376
1684. 8vo. (12°.) London	386
„ 12mo. London	388

218   **British Museum**

		No.
1685.	folio, Oxford	400
„	4to. London	397
1686.	12mo. London	404
1687.	12mo. London	412
„	16mo. London (in shorthand) . . .	413
„	16mo. London, (shorthand, another edition)	413
1688.	folio, Oxford	418
1688.	folio, London	417
„	12mo. London	416
1689.	12mo. London	422
1690.	folio, London	425
„	8vo. London	424
1691.	12mo. Oxford . . .	431
1693.	4to. London	435
1694.	12mo. London	437
1695.	12mo. Oxford	443
1696.	folio, London . . .	444
„	12mo. Edinburgh	449
1697.	4to. Oxford	452
„	12mo. London . . .	450
1698.	12mo. London	454
1698-99.	18mo. London	456
1699.	8vo. London	458
„	12mo. Oxford	460
1700-1699.	4to. Edinburgh . . .	463
1700.	4to. London	464
1701.	folio, London . . .	473
„	folio, Oxford	474
1702.	4to. London	475
„	12mo. London	476
1703.	folio, London . . .	479

	No.
1703. 12mo. London	482
1703-04. 12mo. London	484
1704. 12mo. Oxford	490
1705. 12mo. London	491
1706. folio, London	496
„ 4to. Oxford	499
„ 4to. London	497
1708-06. 12mo. London	504
1708-07. folio	506
„ „ 12mo. London	505
1708. 4to. London	508
„ 4to. London	509
„ 12mo. Oxford	511
1709. folio, London . . .	512
„ 4to. Oxford	514
1711-10. 12mo. London	520

Testaments.

1612. 4to. London, B. L.	6
1619. 24mo. (12°.) London	35
1621. 12mo. London, B. L.	42
1625. 8vo. London	52
1626. 24mo. (12°.) London	57
1627. 12mo. London	60
1628. 8vo. London, B. L.	65
1630. 12mo. London	78
„ 24mo. (12°.) London? (Cambridge 1628)	82
1631. 4to. London, B. L.	88
1633. 8vo. Edinburgh	106
„ 24mo. (12°.) London	102

		No.
1636.	24mo. Edinburgh	125
1638.	24mo. (12°.) London . . .	143
1640.	24mo. (12°.) London	161
„	24mo. (12°.) London	162
1641.	8vo. London, 𝔅. 𝔏.	167
1643.	8vo. Edinburgh, 𝔅. 𝔏. . . .	179
„	12mo. London	178
1648.	8vo. Edinburgh . . .	208
1659.	64mo. London	253
1660.	64mo. London	260
1662.	8vo. Cambridge . . .	268
1664.	12mo. London	274
1680.	4to. Cambridge	352
1683.	4to. London	385
„	8vo. London	380
1691.	8vo. London, 𝔅. 𝔏. . . .	429
„	12mo. Glasgow, 𝔅. 𝔏. . . .	432
1694.	12mo. Edinburgh, 𝔅. 𝔏. . .	439
1696.	8vo. London	446
1699.	12mo. Oxford	462
1700.	32mo. London	470
1704.	8vo. London, 𝔅. 𝔏. . . .	487
„	8vo. London	488
1705.	12mo. London	492
1706.	4to. Oxford	501
1710.	12mo. London	517

Editions of the Authorised Version in Lea Wilson's Catalogue.

As the eſtimate of ſizes in this liſt is made to an arbitrary ſcale and as the ſecond dates are uſually omitted, it has been judged impoſſible to attempt an identification of each edition.

		No. in L. W.
1611. folio, London, 𝔅. 𝔏.	. . . .	112
1612. 4to. London . .	. . .	113
1613. folio, London, 𝔅. 𝔏.	. . .	114
1613. 4to. London, 𝔅. 𝔏.	. . .	115
1614. 4to. London . .	. . .	118
1614. 4to. London, 𝔅. 𝔏.	. . .	119
1614. 8vo. London .	. . .	120
1616. folio, London.	. . .	124
„ 4to. London . .	. . .	125
1617. folio, London, 𝔅. 𝔏.	. .	126
1618. 12mo. London	. .	127
1619. 4to. London, 𝔅. 𝔏.	. . .	128
1620. 4to. London, 𝔅. 𝔏.	. . .	129
„ 12mo. London	. . .	130
1621. 8vo. London .	. . . .	131
1622. 4to. London .	. . . .	132
1623. 8vo. London .	. . . .	133
1625. 4to. London, 𝔅. 𝔏.	. . .	134
„ 12mo. London	. . . .	135
1626. 12mo. London	. . . .	136

		No. in L. W.
1627.	4to. London	137
1628.	4to. London, 𝕭. 𝕷.	138
1629.	folio, Cambridge	139
,,	folio, London	140
1630.	4to. Cambridge, 𝕭. 𝕷.	141
,,	4to. London, 𝕭. 𝕷. . . .	142
,,	4to. London . . .	143
1631.	12mo. London	144
1632.	folio, London . . .	145
,,	4to. London, 𝕭. 𝕷. . .	146
1633.	folio, London	147
,,	8vo. Edinburgh . . .	148
1634.	4to. London, 𝕭. 𝕷. . . .	149
,,	folio, London, 𝕭. 𝕷. . . .	150
,,	8vo. London	151
,,	12mo. London . . .	152
1635.	4to. Cambridge	154
1635.	12mo. London	155
1636.	8vo. London	156
1637.	4to. London	157
,,	4to. Cambridge, 𝕭. 𝕷.	158
,,	12mo. London	159
,,	12mo. London	160
1638.	folio, Cambridge	161
,,	12mo. London	162
1639.	8vo. London	163
1640.	folio, London, 𝕭. 𝕷.	166
,,	4to. London, 𝕭. 𝕷.	167
,,	8vo. London	168
,,	12mo. London	169
1641.	8vo. London	170

		No. in L. W.
1642. folio, Amſterdam	171
1646. 12mo. London	173
,, 8vo. London	174
1647. 8vo. London	175
,, 18mo. London, 𝕭. 𝕷. . .	176
1648. 8vo. London	177
,, 18mo. Cambridge . . .	178
1649. 4to. London	179
,, 12mo. Edinburgh and London . .	180
1650. 12mo. London	181
1651. 8vo. London	182
1653. 18mo. London . . .	183
,, 24mo. London . . .	184
,, 24mo. London . . .	185
,, 12mo. London . . .	186
,, 24mo. London . . .	187
1654. 4to. London . . .	188
1655. 12mo. London (Field) . . .	189
,, 12mo. London (Tyler) . . .	190
1657. 8vo. Cambridge . . .	191
,, 12mo. London . . .	192
,, 18mo. London . . .	193
1658. 24mo. London . . .	194
,, 24mo. London . . .	195
1660. folio, Cambridge . . .	196
,, 8vo. London . . .	197
,, 12mo. London . . .	198
1661. 8vo. Cambridge . . .	199
,, 4to. London . . .	200
1664. 12mo. (Amſterdam) . . .	201
1666. 18mo. London . . .	202

		No. in L. W.
1668. 4to. Cambridge		203
1669. 12mo. London		204
1671. 12mo. London		205
„ 8vo. London		206
1672. folio, Amſterdam		207
1674. folio, Cambridge		208
„ 24mo. London		209
1676. 8vo. Edinburgh		210
„ 8vo. London		211
„ 24mo. London		212
1679. 4to. Oxford		213
„ 8vo. London		214
1682. folio, Oxford		215
„ 12mo. (Amſterdam) . . .		216
1683. folio. (Amſterdam)		217
1684. 12mo. London		218
1684. 12mo. London		219
1688. folio, Oxford		220
1689. 18mo. London		221
1691. 24mo. Oxford		222
1694. 12mo. Edinburgh		223
1695. 18mo. Oxford		224
1696. 18mo. Edinburgh		225
1698. 12mo. London		226
„ 24mo. Edinburgh		227
1704. 18mo. Oxford		228
1706. folio, London		229
1708. folio, (Amſterdam)		230
1711. 18mo. London		231

Lea Wilſon's Teſtaments of the Authoriſed Verſion.

Q

		No. in L. W.
1686.	12mo. Glafgow, 𝔅. 𝔏.	92
1691.	12mo. Glafgow, 𝔅. 𝔏.	93
1694.	18mo. Edinburgh, 𝔅. 𝔏. . .	94
1700.	12mo. Amfterdam	95
„	12mo. Amfterdam	96

𝔅𝔦𝔟𝔩𝔢𝔰 𝔬𝔣 𝔱𝔥𝔢 𝔄𝔲𝔱𝔥𝔬𝔯𝔦𝔰𝔢𝔡 𝔙𝔢𝔯𝔰𝔦𝔬𝔫 𝔦𝔫 𝔱𝔥𝔢 𝔏𝔞𝔪𝔟𝔢𝔱𝔥 𝔏𝔦𝔟𝔯𝔞𝔯𝔶.

		No.
1611.	folio, fecond iffue, London, 𝔅. 𝔏. . .	2
1617.	folio, London, 𝔅. 𝔏.	27
1629.	folio, the New Teftament, printed only on one fide, Cambridge	72
1634.	folio, London, 𝔅. 𝔏.	109
1638.	folio, Cambridge	145
1657.	8vo. Cambridge	247
1660.	8vo. London	257
1663.	4to. Cambridge	269
1700.	4to. London	464
1701.	folio, London	473

𝔅𝔦𝔟𝔩𝔢𝔰 𝔞𝔫𝔡 𝔑𝔢𝔴 𝔗𝔢𝔰𝔱𝔞𝔪𝔢𝔫𝔱𝔰 𝔦𝔫 𝔆𝔞𝔫𝔱𝔢𝔯𝔟𝔲𝔯𝔶 𝔆𝔞𝔱𝔥𝔢𝔡𝔯𝔞𝔩 𝔏𝔦𝔟𝔯𝔞𝔯𝔶.

The majority of thefe Bibles are the property of the Venerable Archdeacon Harrifon.

1611.	folio, fecond iffue, imperfect, 𝔅. 𝔏. . .	2
1614-15.	4to. London, 𝔅. 𝔏.	18
1618-17.	12mo. London	31
1630.	4to. Cambridge, 𝔅. 𝔏.	81

Bodleian Library, Oxford.

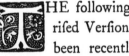HE following editions of the Autho-rifed Verfion have, for the moft part been recently acquired, and as the collection is being almoft daily added to, it may be well to fay that the enumeration was made on the 15th February, 1872. A line of acknowledgment is due to the kindnefs of the Librarian and his affiftants, without which it would have been impoffible to complete the lift. Many examples of this

verfion are to be found in College Libraries
as well as in the Public Library at Cambridge
and in that of Trinity College, Dublin ; but
the collection at the Bodleian is by far the
moft important, both in fize and in the rarity
of the editions which it contains.

Folio.

	No.
1611. Firft iffue: engraved title, London, 𝕭. 𝕷. .	1
„ Second iffue : (imperf.) London, 𝕭. 𝕷. .	2
1613-11. London, 𝕭. 𝕷.	7
1613. London, 𝕭. 𝕷.	10
1616. London	24
1617. London, 𝕭. 𝕷.	27
1629. London	68
„ London	68
„ Cambridge	72
1633-32. London	97
1634. London, 𝕭. 𝕷.	109
1638. Cambridge	145
1639-38-39. London	148
„ „ „ London	148
1640-39. London, 𝕭. 𝕷.	154
1660-59. Cambridge	256
1672. (Amfterdam)	297
1674. Cambridge	310
1679. London (Amfterdam)	343
1682. Oxford	369
1683. (Amfterdam)	384

No.

1688. Oxford 418
1708. (Amſterdam) 507

𝕼𝖚𝖆𝖗𝖙𝖔.

1612. London 4
1613-12. London 8
1613. London, 𝕭. 𝕷. 11
1613-14. London, 𝕭. 𝕷. 14
1614-15. London, 𝕭. 𝕷. 18
1619-20. London, 𝕭. 𝕷. 36
1622-22-23. London 44
1625-25-24. London, 𝕭. 𝕷. 49
1628. London, 𝕭. 𝕷. 62
1630. London, 𝕭. 𝕷. 73
„ Cambridge 80
„ Cambridge, 𝕭. 𝕷. 81
1633. London 98
„ Cambridge, 𝕭. 𝕷. 103
1634. London, 𝕭. 𝕷. 110
„ another copy, 𝕭. 𝕷. 110
1637. London 126
„ Cambridge 130
1639. Cambridge, 𝕭. 𝕷. 152
1645. 186
1648. London 199
„ London, (Field) 203
„ London, (Field) 203
1649. London 210
1654-53. London 229

		No.
1654. London	. . . . .	230
1655. London	. . . . .	232
1663. Cambridge	. . . .	269
1666. Cambridge	. . . .	278
1668-66. Cambridge	. . . .	279
1670. Cambridge	. . .	288
1673. Cambridge	. . . .	302
1675. Cambridge	. . . .	314
1675-75-73. Oxford	. . .	311
1677. Cambridge	. .	327
1678. London	. . . .	329
„ Another edition	. .	330
1679. Oxford	. . .	340
„ Variation edition	. . . .	341
1682. Oxford	. . . .	370
1683. Oxford	. .	383
„ Cambridge	. .	382
1685. London	. . . .	394
1686. Oxford	. . .	406
„ Another copy.	. . .	406
1697. Oxford.	. . . .	452
1700. London	. . .	464
1702. London	. . . .	475
1703. London	. . . .	480
„ Oxford.	. . .	483
1706. London	. . . .	497

Octavo and Duodecimo.

1612. London, 8vo.	. . . . .	5
1614. London, 8vo.	. . . . .	17

		No.
1617. London, 8vo.		28
1619. London (imperfeck), 8vo. . . .		33
1622. London, 8vo.		43
1625. London, 12mo.		51
1631. London, 8vo.		84
1632-31. London, 12mo.		92
1633. London, 12mo.		100
„ Edinburgh, 8vo.		104
1636. London, 8vo.		123
1638. London, 12mo.		140
1639. London, 8vo.		151
1640. London, 8vo.		158
„ Another edition, 8vo.		159
1642. London, 12mo.		169
1643. London, 8vo.		176
1646-48. London, 8vo.		191, 202
1647. London, 8vo.		193
1648-46. London, 8vo.		202, 191
1648. London, 8vo.		200
„ Cambridge, 12mo.		205
„ Cambridge, 12mo.		206
1650. London, 8vo.		214
1651-50. London, 8vo.		216
1651. London, 12mo.		217
1653. London, 12mo.		221
„ London, 12mo.		222
1654. London, 12mo.		231
„ London, 12mo.		234
1655. London, 12mo.		236
1660. London, 8vo.		257
„ London, 12mo.		259

		No.
1661. Cambridge, 8vo.		264
1664. (Amſterdam,) 12mo. . . .		272
1666. London, 12mo.		277
1669. London, 12mo.		283
1670-71. London, 8vo.		290
1670-75. London, 8vo. . . .		291
1671. London, 8vo. . . .		294
1672. London, 12mo.		295
1673. London, 12mo.		300
„ London, 12mo.		301
1676. London, 12mo.		319
1679. London, 8vo.		335
„ London, 12mo. . . .		337
1680. London, 12mo.		350
1681. London, 12mo. . . .		358
1682. London, 12mo. . . .		367
1684. London, 12mo. . . .		386
„ Another copy. 12mo. . .		386
1688. Oxford, 12mo.		420
1689. London, 12mo.		422
„ Another copy, uncut. 12mo. . .		422
„ Oxford, 8vo.		423
1692. Oxford, 12mo.		433
1694. London, 12mo. . . .		437
1695. Oxford, 12mo. . . .		443
„ Another copy. 12mo. . . .		443
1696. Oxford, 12mo.		448
1698. Edinburgh, 12mo. . . .		455
1698-96. London, 12mo. . . .		453
1699. London, 12mo.		459
1700. London, 12mo.		465

The Collection of Francis Fry, Efq., F.S.A.

HIS is by far the moft extenfive collection of Englifh Bibles of all verfions in England. Owing to the kindnefs and perfonal help of Mr. Fry, the following lift has been compiled from the vaft ftore of materials in his hands: it is right however to fay that it by no means exhaufts his library, and can only be taken as a large felection. In the cafe of fome editions Mr. Fry has been able to identify as many as feven different iffues and to fhow two and even three copies of each, whilft the examples he poffeffes of others are not unfrequently unique fo far as it is poffible to decide at prefent.

𝕱𝖔𝖑𝖎𝖔.

	No.
1611. First iſſue. London, 𝕭. 𝕷. . . .	1
„　Second iſſue. London, 𝕭. 𝕷. .	2
„　Reprints. London, 𝕭. 𝕷. . . .	—
„　Reprints, differing. London, 𝕭. 𝕷. .	—
1613-11. London, 𝕭. 𝕷.	7
1613. London, 𝕭. 𝕷.	10
1614-17. London, 𝕭. 𝕷.	19
1616. London	24
1617. London, 𝕭. 𝕷.	27
1629. London	68
„　Cambridge	72
1632. London . . .	93
1633-32-32. London	97
1634. (On toned paper.) London, 𝕭. 𝕷. .	109
1638. London	138
1638. Cambridge . . .	145
1638-39. London	148
1640-39. London, 𝕭. 𝕷. . . .	154
1642-3. Amſterdam	175
1644. Amſterdam	182
1672. Amſterdam	297
1679. (Amſterdam) . . .	344
1682. Oxford	369
„　Oxford	369
1683. (Amſterdam).	384
1684. Oxford	390
1688. Oxford	418
1706. London	496
1708-07. (Amſterdam)	506
1709. London	512

Quarto.

		No.
1612. London	. . . . . .	4
1613-12. London .	. . . .	8
„ London, B. L.	. . . . .	11
1613. London	. . . . .	12
1613-14. London, B. L. .	. . . .	14
1614-12-13. London	. . . .	16
1614-15. London, B. L. .	. . .	18
1616. London	. . . .	25
1619-14. London, B. L. .	. . . .	36
1619. London	. . . . .	32
1619-20. London, B. L. .	. . . .	36
1620-21. London, B. L. .	. . . .	40
1622-23. London	. . . . .	44
1625-24. London, B. L. .	. . . .	49
1625. London, B. L.	. . . .	49
1627. London	. . . . .	58
1628. London, B. L.	. . . .	62
1629. London	. . . . .	69
1630. London, B. L.	. . . . .	73
„ London, B. L.	. . . . .	74
„ London .	. . . . .	75
„ Cambridge, B. L. .	. . . .	81
1632-30. London .	. . . .	90
1632-31. London, B. L. .	. . . .	91
„ „ London, B. L. .	. . . .	91
1633. Cambridge, B. L. .	. . . .	103
„ Cambridge, B. L. .	. . . .	103
1633-34. London	. . . . .	108
1634. London, B. L.	. . . . .	110
„ London, B. L.	. . . . .	110

	No.
1634. London, 𝔅. 𝔏. . . .	110
1634-36-34. London, 𝔅. 𝔏. . . .	110
1635. Cambridge . . .	119
1637. Cambridge	130
,, ,, London	135
,, ,, London	135
1637-38. Cambridge . . .	137
,, ,, Cambridge . . .	137
,, London, 𝔅. 𝔏. . . .	150
1639. Cambridge, 𝔅. 𝔏.	152
1640-41-42. London, 𝔅. 𝔏. . . .	164
1645.	186
1648. London	199
,, London	203
,, London	203
1649. London	210
1654-53. London	229
1655. London	232
1661. London	263
,, London	263
1663. Cambridge	269
1668-66. Cambridge . . .	279
1670. Cambridge	288
1673. Cambridge	302
1675-73. Oxford	311
1675. Oxford	311
1676. London	320
1677-75. Cambridge . . .	323
1678. London	329
1679. Oxford	340
,, Oxford	341

					No.
1682-80. Cambridge	.	.	.	.	365
1683. Cambridge	.	.	.	.	382
1685. London	.	.	.	.	394
1697. Oxford.	.	.	.	.	452
1700. London	.	.	.	.	464
1705. Edinburgh	.	.	.	.	494
1708. London	.	.	.	.	509

Octavo.

1612. London	.	.	.	.	.	5
,, London	.	.	.	.		5
1613-12. London	.	.	.		.	9
1613. London	.	.	.	.	.	13
1614. London	.	.	.	.	.	17
1615. London	.	.	.	.	.	21
1617. London	.	.	.		.	28
1618. London	.	.	.	.	.	30
1619-18. London	.	.	.	.	.	33
1620. London	.	.	.	.	.	38
1621. London	.	.	.	.	.	41
1622. London	.	.	.	.	.	43
1624. London	.	.	.	.	.	47
1625. London	.	.	.	.	.	50
,, . .	.	.	.	.	.	50
1626. London	.	.	.	.	.	54
,, London	.	.	.	.	.	54
1627. London	.	.	.	.	.	59
1628. London	.	.	.	.	.	63
,, London	.	.	.	.	.	63
,, London	.	.	.	.	.	63
1629. London	.	.	.	.	.	70

		No.
1653. London	. . . . . .	222
,, London	. . . . . .	223
,, London	. . . . . .	224
,, London	. . . . . .	225
1654. London	. . . . . .	231
1655. London	. . . . . .	234
,, London	. . . . . .	236
1656-55. London	. . . . . .	237
1657-56. London	. . . . . .	241
,, ,, London	. . . . . .	242
1657-58. London	. . . . . .	248
1658. London	. . . . . .	250
,, London	. . . . . .	250
,, London	. . . . . .	251
,, London	. . . . . .	251
1660. London	. . . . . .	259
1661-60. London	. . . . . .	262
,, ,, London	. . . . . .	262
1664. London	. . . . . .	274
,, .	. . . . . .	272
1665-62. London	. . . . , .	275
1668. London	. . . . . .	280
1669. London	. . . . .	283
1672. London	. . . . . .	295
1672-73. London	. . . . . .	298
1673. London	. . . . . .	301
,, Edinburgh	. . . . .	303
1674. London	. . . . . .	306
1675. London	. . . . . .	313
,, Edinburgh	. . . . .	315
1676. London	. . . . . .	319

The Collection of

No.

		No.
1676. London	. . . . . .	319
1679. London	. . . . . .	337
1680. London	. . . . . .	350
1680-84. London	. . . . . .	357
1681. London	. . . . . .	360
„ London	. . . . . .	360
„ Oxford	. . . . . .	362
1682. London	. . . . . .	367
„	. . . . . .	373
„	. . . . . .	374
1683. London	. . . .	379
1684. London	. . . .	386
„ London	. . . . . .	387
„ London	. . . . . .	388
„ London	. . . . . .	389
1684-85. London	. . . . . .	393
1685. London	. . . . . .	396
1685-86. Oxford	. . . . . .	402
1686. London	. . . . . .	404
„ Oxford	. . . . . .	408
1686-87. Oxford	. . . . . .	410
1688. London	. . . . . .	416
1691. London	. . . . . .	427
„ London	. . . . . .	428
„ Oxford	. . . . . .	430
„ Oxford	. . . . . .	431
1693-91. London	. . . . . .	434
1695. London	. . . . . .	440
„ Oxford	. . . . . .	443
1696. Oxford	. . . . . .	448

No.

1698. London 454

,, Edinburgh 455

1698-99. London 456

1698-1700. London 457

1703. London 482

1704. London 486

1705. London 491

1706. London 498

1706. Oxford 500

1707. Oxford 503

1708. Oxford 511

1710. Edinburgh 518

1711. London 522

,, Oxford 524

𝕿𝖊𝖘𝖙𝖆𝖒𝖊𝖓𝖙𝖘.

1612. London, 𝕭. 𝕷. 4to. 6

1621. London, 𝕭. 𝕷. 12mo. 42

1622. London, 𝕭. 𝕷. 12mo. 45

,, London, 32mo. 52

1625. London, 𝕭. 𝕷. 12mo. 53

1627. London, 𝕭. 𝕷. 12mo. 61

1631. London, 𝕭. 𝕷. 4to. 88

,, London, 𝕭. 𝕷. 12mo. 89

1633. Edinburgh, 8vo. or 12mo. . . . 105

1635. London, 𝕭. 𝕷. 8vo. 116

,, Edinburgh, 𝕭. 𝕷. 12mo. . . . 120

1638. London, 𝕭. 𝕷. 12mo. 142

,, London, 12mo. fmall 143

1647. London, 𝕭. 𝕷. 12mo. 196

1648. London, 12mo. 204

No.

1653. London, 8vo.	227
1656. London, 12mo.	239
1659. London, 12mo.	254
1676. London, 8vo.	321
1684. Amſterdam, 12mo.	392
1686. London, 8vo.	405
1691. Glaſgow, 12mo.	432
1700. London, 12mo.	466
„ Amſterdam, 12mo.	469
1704. London, 12mo.	489

BIBLES OF THE AUTHORISED VERSION
IN THE ROYAL LIBRARY,
STUTTGART.

HIS lift is added by the kindnefs of the Rev. Sir William Cope, Bart., by whom it was compiled in 1859. I have not ventured to number the lift, as I have had no opportunity of feeing the collection, and I have left off at 1711.

Folio.	*Quarto.*
1613. London.	1612. N. T. London.
1629. Cambridge.	1613. London.
„ London.	1614. „
1634. „	1619. „
1638. „	1620. „
1674. Cambridge.	1630. „
1679. Amfterdam.	1631. N. T. London.
1682. Oxford.	1633. Cambridge.
1683. London.	1634. London.
„ No place or name.	1637. Cambridge.
1701. Oxford.	1640. London.
1703. London.	1645. (Amfterdam ?)
1706. London.	1648. London.

1649. London.
1663. Cambridge.
1668. ,,
1677-76. London.
1677. Cambridge.
1678. London.
1679. Oxford.
1683. Cambridge.
1697. London.
   ,, Oxford.
1702. London.
1703. London.

Octavo et infra.
1614. London.
1619.   ,,
1623.   ,,
1625.   ,,
1627. N. T. Lond. 16mo.
1628. London.
1629. N. T. only London.
1631-30. London.
1636. London, 32mo.
1637.   ,,
1638.   ,,
   ,,   ,,
1640. N. T. London.
1641. London.
1642.   ,,
1643. N. T. Edinburgh.
1645. Amſterdam.

1645. London.
1646. N.T.London,𝕭.𝕷.(?)
1647. London.
1648. Cambridge, 8vo.
   ,,   ,,   12mo.
1650. London.
1651.   ,,   imperf.
1652.   ,,
1653.   ,,   large 12mo.
1653. London, 12mo.
   ,,   ,,   16mo.
   ,, N.T.London, 16mo.
1654. N.T.   ,,
1655. London.
   ,,   ,,
1657. Cambridge.
1658.   ,,   16mo.
1660. London.
   ,,   ,,   ſmaller.
1661. London.
   ,, Cambridge.
1663. London.
   ,, Cambridge.
1664. N. T. London.
1668-70. London.
1669.   ,,
1670.   ,,
1671. N. T. London.
1673. London, large 8vo.
1677. London.
1679.   ,,

1680. Oxford.
1681-83. London, 16mo.
1682-79.　„　　large 8vo.
1682-89.　„　large 12mo.
1684.　　　„
　　„　　　„
1685. Oxford.
1686. London.
1687.　　„　　12mo.
1688. Oxford, 12mo.
1689. London.
　„　N. T. Oxford.
1690-91. London.
1694. London, imperf. 8vo.

1694. O. T. Edinb., N. T.
　　　　　Lond., 12mo.
1695. London, large 12mo.
　„　Oxford, large 12mo.
1696. London.
1698. London.
1699. London.
1700-01. Edinburgh.
1702. London, 12mo.
1703-00. Oxford.
1704. N. T. Oxford.
　„　N. T. London.
1708. London.